God bless you

Quinie

www.iamthehax.
com

Donations

Before the Lights Go Out

Eleven Keys to Achieving
Real Physical Intimacy

By

Quiniece Sheppard

All Scripture quotations, unless otherwise indicated, are taken from the Holy Bible: Woman Thou Art Loosed Edition by T.D. Jakes, New King James Version. Copyright © 1998 by Thomas Nelson, Inc. Used by permission. All rights reserved.

ISBN 0-7414-6535-3

Printed in the United States of America

Published May 2011

INFINITY PUBLISHING
1094 New DeHaven Street, Suite 100
West Conshohocken, PA 19428-2713
Toll-free (877) BUY BOOK
Local Phone (610) 941-9999
Fax (610) 941-9959
Info@buybooksontheweb.com
www.buybooksontheweb.com

TABLE OF CONTENTS

ACKNOWLEDGMENTS

To God be the Glory. My Lord and Savior, we did it again and I couldn't have done it without You. I prayed and You answered. I cried and You dried my tears away. I suffered and You healed. I doubted and You strengthened my faith. I got worried and stressed out and You gave me peace. Thank you Jesus for being there with me every step of the way because I know You was there. If it had not been for You, I would still be lost and going around circles in the wilderness, but I surely thank You for making the crooked path straight. You gave me gifts I never knew I had and I hope to use all of my gifts to Your glory. I love you Jesus so much. You are everything to me, literally.

To my mother, Annie Lee, and my father, Vermon Sheppard, thanks for your continual support and encouragement. I will never forget the sacrifices that both of you made so I could be where I am today. Mom, thanks for all the years you worked in the fields so that I could have the necessary tools that I needed to function in life. Dad, thanks for making me go to Sunday school every Sunday. It definitely gave me the Christian foundation that I needed to grow closer to God. I know one day soon that I will be able to take care of you guys, the same way you took care of me. Love you both from the bottom of my heart.

To my twelve brothers and sisters: Sherry Dawkins, Cassandra Sheppard, Delancy Melton, Fitzgerald Sheppard, Alvin Sheppard, Burnett

Sheppard, Teonna Mills, Ronnie Sheppard, Gene Sheppard, Marlena Lewis, Pamela Sheppard, and Kelsey Sheppard. Thanks for all the love and support, and your faith in me. It really means a lot to me knowing that I have each of you in my corner. I am pressing forward because you all give me the incentive to do so. A special thank you to those who shared their testimonies for this book. You all are the best siblings a girl could ever have. Love you all.

To my seventeen nieces and nephews: I am honored to be called your auntie. I had the special privilege and challenge of babysitting most of you. Let's just say, "We've had some good days and we've had some bad days," but I am not complaining. Laugh Out Loud. (LOL) Each of you bring joy to my soul and I hope that I can spend more time with each of you than I have in the past. Auntie loves you all dearly.

To my closest friends and you know who you are: Each of you has brought something unique into my life. With many of you, I have cried, laughed and shared my innermost thoughts and feelings, and you all were right there listening, praying and pushing me forward. I appreciate you all so much for 'ridin' with me. We have had many fun moments together and they are too many to name. Thanks so much for your continual support and encouragement. It is important to have a strong knit relationship with people, who are in your network or circle of friends that keep you focused and grounded in the Lord. I appreciate you all. Also, thanks to two dear friends who shared with me words of wisdom. I was able to use a lot of what I learned from you in this book. You didn't know it at the time, but you really helped me write this book. You all are the best. Love you dearly.

Thanks to my editor, Adrienna Turner: Wow. You did such an awesome job with developing this book. There are so many things that I left out or overlooked that you brought to my attention. It really showed me how much you value your work. Moreover, it is good to have a Christian editor who prays and seeks God about every line, every sentence, and every paragraph that you read. What you do is not only a gift, but a ministry. I appreciate your efforts and hard work you put into this project. It would not be what it is without your expertise. God bless you.

A very special thank you to my dear sister, Teonna Mills, who added additional edits to this book. Thank you so much sis for your insight and encouragement. You pointed out so many different things that I didn't see and helped me out a great deal. You definitely kept it real with me and I needed that. You are truly a gift to me and I wouldn't have done this without your additional help and assistance. We make a great team. A third book is coming your way shortly. LOL! Love you bunches.

Thanks to my hair designer and makeup artist Vetrice Barry. Girl, you have done it again. From the hair to the makeup, you can do it all. I appreciate you for bringing out the very best in me and helping me to shine in my uniqueness. Thank you so much for everything. Love you.

To my photographer, Eric Barry, you were awesome. Once again, I had another great photo shoot. You definitely know what works and what doesn't work, and have a gift of working with clients to meet their individual needs. Keep working your gift as God will definitely elevate you to new heights. Thanks so much. Love you.

A heartfelt thank you to my pastor James Nelson and my first lady Wendy Nelson for the tremendous amount of support and encouragement you have shown me as God knows it helped me at such a time when I was feeling very low and in despair. After experiencing rejection, sadness and depression, you came right on time and I mean that literally. I'm better because of you and I feel better too. I know without a doubt that God lead me to you both. I thank God for the both of you every chance I get. You both are great individuals who are sincere, loving and very down to earth and I love that trait about the both of you. It's a rarity. Trust me. Thanks so much for everything. The best is yet to come. I'm excited about my destiny at Destiny Christian Church. Love you both dearly.

Lastly, thanks to every single person who purchased this book. I hope it blessed you in your relationships and I hope you participate in the six month covenant challenge as a way to strengthen your commitment to God. I am grateful for the opportunity to minister God's Word to you in the many different avenues that He has called me to do. I am inspired to write, speak and do the many things God has called me to do, as difficult the tasks as they are, because of my love for God and for you. You all are so easy to love. Thanks for loving me back. Continue to pray for me and I will do the same for you. To my single sistas, I got your back! We are in this together. Stay strong and empowered. Love you all.

PREFACE

Many of you read the title of this book and assumed it is another book about sex, and that you have read books like this one before countless times. They're all saying one thing- sex is the most important factor in having a long-lasting relationship; therefore, you need to know how to please your mate in the bedroom. Am I right? Reading that statement sounded like an infomercial, didn't it? The title of the book suggests it's a book about sex, but the book is NOT about sex, at least not in the way you think. Yes, you and I will talk about sex, but it's not about sex. Does that make sense? If it doesn't make sense right now, then it will before you finish reading this book and you'll say, "oh, okay, now I get what she was talking about."

This book is primarily written to the woman about the man. I'm primarily writing from the perspective of a woman giving her some pointers and tips. Steve Harvey did a similar thing in his book, *Act like a Lady, Think like a Man*, in which he wrote his book from a man's perspective to the woman. The major difference between my book and Harvey's is that my book is written from a Christian perspective and his was written from a worldly point of view. When I began writing this book, Harvey's wasn't published yet and the moment I heard of his book and read it, I knew why God wanted me to write this book. God had me write this book at such a time as this when relationships are dissolving at an alarming rate and promiscuity is seen as normal behavior. This book is so timely and relevant and these principles are so basic, yet so many of them are missed or overlooked in our relationships. It's simple, but effective. It's not deep, but thought-provoking. Lastly, it's not gender specific. Everyone can benefit from reading this book.

For single women, this book is a guide to help choose the ideal man for a queen like you because any man just won't do. In other words, the person you are dating, what is he "bringing to the table"? For married couples, this book will act as a guide to determine what is missing in your marriage and how couples can put the pieces back together again. Therefore, this is a relational book, for those who are single, as well as for those who are in a committed relationship, divorced, widowed or married. This book will take you to a deeper level of understanding about how God views marriages. It will also allow you to examine your habits, behaviors, and mindsets including evaluating your past relationships, both introspectively and retrospectively. There are some things you need to know "before you turn off the lights" and what foreplay is all about.

Ladies, I want you to read this book as if you and I are having a conversation and I am sitting right there beside you on the sofa because this is such a relatable book. The correct term to use for this type of book is called self-help, which is a book designed to provide you with tools to help you become a better person. In other words, it is to help *you* work on *you*. I know you and I can both agree that there's always room for improvement in certain areas of our lives whether it be health, finances, spiritual growth, family, relationships, etc and I intend on helping you improve two of the above areas: spiritual growth and relationships.

So, in order to help you, I want you to broaden your way of thinking and keep an open mind and by the middle of this book, you will have a different mindset. If you are open to receive, you will receive. It's that simple. I'm sure that after you read this book, you will make comments like, "Hmm," "very interesting," or "it does make sense." Many of you will learn something new, while others will be motivated to take what they already know and apply it in their relationships. Either way, implementation and application are what need to happen after you read this book.

Quickly, go and grab some popcorn and a cup of tea and get a note pad and a pen so you can take notes. Ladies, let's begin our girls roundtable discussion. The rest of you can eavesdrop on our discussion and take notes. Actually, you'll be in some parts of the conversation as well as I talk to all of you at some points in the book. Since I love to talk, I'll break the ice and start the conversation.

INTRODUCTION

Sex is a popular topic in our society today. Don't you agree? Sex sells. Sex is displayed on bulletin boards, magazines, and television commercials. In addition, sex is glorified and written in some literature. Sex is also exposed in the music videos, pornography sites on the Internet, and late night cartoons such as Adult Swim, television shows, and radio programs. We see how people are dressed, and contestants on dance shows are half-dressed, but all these images we see are false. Don't believe the hype. Inevitably, sex should be taken way more seriously than the images we see portrayed in the media. Sex can be deadly physically, emotionally and spiritually because every time we engage in pre-marital sex, a piece of us dies. We'll talk more about the emotional and spiritual death later on in the book. We treat sex like we are playing Russian roulette. The more people we sleep with, the more likely we will die from HIV or AIDS and other STDs. This is where the physical death comes in.

My main objectives are to tell everyone what sex means to God, and how we should feel about sex based on the Word of God. Is sex enjoyable or is it boring? Does sex leave us fulfilled, empty, or lonely after it's over? While we are having sex, are we lying there waiting for it to be over or wishing it would last longer? The reason I ask these questions is because it seems that no one is asking them. We can be so caught up in the act itself that we disregard the motives behind the act. Some of us are having sex because it is what everyone else is doing. Others think because you're dating, then sex comes with the territory. In other words, you are *obligated* to have sex.

Okay, go back and think about the questions I posed. I also want you to think about the person(s) you are sleeping with and see what types of conclusions you draw. The preceding and the following questions all relate to intimacy. What is your relationship with the person you are sleeping with and what type of connection or bond do you have with that person? Have you established a spiritual and emotional connection with that person? Does having a physical connection mean there's intimacy in your relationship, or is it that you are just being physical with one another? Ah ha! I know I am making someone raise his eyebrows right now and say, "Where in the world is she going with this?"

> Physical connection with someone does not mean there's intimacy in your relationship. Examine your relationship to determine what type of connection or bond you have with him/her.

Sex is a physical act and it is physical intimacy, or is it? Well, you and I need to clear some things up about intimacy, which is what this book is all about. Do we need to have intimate feelings for our mate to engage in foreplay? I will give brief descriptions on intimacy, and then I will discuss different levels of foreplay to improve the level of intimacy in our relationships. Lastly, I will pose a challenge for all the single men and women that will motivate and inspire them to change their current sexual habits by changing the way they view sex. You have your note pad and pen right? You will need it so you can jot things down and answer the thought-provoking questions at the end of each chapter. Yes, you are going to do a little homework, not for anyone else to grade, but so you can grade yourselves to see where you are and whether you are passing or failing. If you are failing in your relationships, then hopefully you will pass after you finish reading this book and put what you have learned into practice.

To develop physical intimacy, women need foreplay. Women like to be warmed up before they get to the main course. Women like attention and affection. These eleven principles are what need to happen "before the lights go out." There are many marriages or relationships that have problems because they have no clue what foreplay is. Foreplay will draw the two of you closer together, forming a bond that is difficult to be broken. This is what women really want—a relationship that lasts and endures. Leave the lights on a little longer and follow these eleven principles to a rewarding relationship. Ladies, are you ready? Gentleman, stay with me. Married couples, stay focused so you can help your friends out. Ha, Ha. I got something for you couples as well. In this book, we all will come out better, stronger and wiser.

INTIMACY

Before we get into the eleven principles, let's first talk about intimacy because this will help us put these principles into practice. What is intimacy? First, let's take a closer look at the word. In-ti-ma-cy translates to mean "in to me." Do you see that? This is where the person you're dating is able to know your thoughts, feelings, goals, dreams, desires, and so forth. In other words, he has an emotional and spiritual connection with you. Some would say, "I've found my soul mate." A *soul mate* is someone who you share commonalities with and have the same beliefs and attitudes. Once you establish a mutual liking towards one another, you are emotionally-bonded to the person you are "into" and that emotional bonding attaches to your soul, thus forming a soul tie. Yes, we are going to go there!

A marriage is a soul tie as the bible states that two shall become one. In other words, two souls are linked together to become as one. Any relationships outside of marriage, (fornication) and against God's will (disobedience) is what I call an illegal soul tie. Uh oh. It's getting ready to get tight now. (I talk about illegal soul ties in my first book, *The Seven Deadly Sexual Sins*) If God hasn't put the two of you together, then your relationship is illegal, meaning it is not ordained by God nor is it in His will. There are so many relationships that are dissolving because people are tied to the wrong person. Be careful who you link up to as linking up with the wrong person can break you spiritually, emotionally and also physically.

Remember as children we played this game called Red Rover. There were two teams comprised of ten or more people who would join hands, face each other and stand in two lines. (This was played outdoors) Someone would go first and choose a person who they thought was weak and fragile to charge through the opposite line from the one you were standing in to break or separate those who were joined hands. You would say, "red rover, red rover, send Tiffany right over". Y'all remember that game? If you broke through the joined hands in the circle, then those hands that you broke through were part of your team. If you didn't break through those hands that you tried to break through, then they stayed in their line. You would do this until there were no more joined hands to break through and there was a single line. Well, what's my point? My point is that you betta be locked or joined to another strong hand because if you aren't, then the relationship will break or fall apart. If you are connected to the right hand, then your relationship will not be easily broken. As we go through this book, I hope you will shake yourself loose from an illegal soul tie and allow God to tie you to the right one, which is your soul mate. The tie has a knot in it, so you can't easily take it apart. That's the type of relationship you should strive to obtain. Okay, we got a little sidetracked, so back to the conversation.

How do I know if the relationship is serious enough, where couples can take it to the next level—engagement? Well, I'm glad you asked. Before you can be physically intimate with someone, you have to be mentally and spiritually connected. If all you have in common with the opposite sex is sex, then all you have is sex without the intimacy. Two people can have sex.

Yet, the question arises: Is sex physical intimacy or is it just physical?

> Sex without intimacy is just a physical encounter, not a relationship.

In society, we view the term, *physical intimacy* as someone having sexual relations or being sexual with someone because there is an exchange of emotions and bodily fluids. However, couples can experience *empty exchanges*, where one feels empty, lonely, unfulfilled, unloved, unwanted and undesired, even after sex. Wow! I thought that sex was supposed to make me feel good and wanted. Well, here's the deal. Ladies, let's say that you meet a young man who shows you the attention and affection you're seeking, but don't give it to you. In other words, *giving* is an *inward* expression, whereas *showing* is an *outward* expression. For example, he can buy you flowers, candy, cards, etc. as an outward expression of showing that he loves you, but not necessarily meeting your spiritual and emotional needs, which requires giving. Consequently, showing ignores the thoughtfulness and consideration in which the woman longs for. Basically, he spends his money on you, instead of the quality time that it takes to get to know you. Others would say that he is not "into you." He meets your wants, but not your needs. In other words, you want flowers, gifts, pedicures, manicures, candy and dates, but those things are tangible. They can be replaced. However, what about meeting your spiritual and emotional needs?

Overall, women desire to be loved, cared for, appreciated, valued, and to feel special. Consequently, he is showing the woman that he loves her, and she also desires to feel needed. In the relationship, couples need to express love by showing and giving to one another. You can endow your mate with gifts and also spend quality time and affection with the person you love. Giving requires time, effort, energy, and consideration. I'm talking about putting in the time that it takes to get to know someone, for real. Aside from the gifts, candy, money and dates, a lady needs a man to be into her and discover what type of person she really is.

Showing is an outward expression of love. *Giving* is an inward expression of love. You need to have both to have a solid, healthy relationship.

Money cannot replace intimacy and cannot buy love. If someone had all the money in the world, he still would be looking for love elsewhere because loving someone is more of an inward expression than it is outward. We have to connect with our emotional and spiritual side for real intimacy to take place.

We have confused intimacy with sex. This is why there are sexual perversions today. We have many sexual partners because we have not realized that sex does not make a relationship. Some of us focus on the good sex that we've had with our partner, but cannot get along with him. We have our differences. We argue all the time. We disagree about everything. We have completely different outlooks on our goals and dreams. We then realize that the both of us are on two separate pages in the chapter of life. The problem is that we have no bond or true intimacy in our relationship. When the sex is over, women need someone whom they can talk to, and who will listen. Women need someone whom they can laugh with, or cry with. Women desire someone who shares common interests and similarities. Moreover, women want to be with someone whom they can spend their lives with and learn from. These things are what intimacy is about. When we have sex before developing intimacy, then all we have is just sex. Does this make sense to you? Am I helping you discover what intimacy is really about? Let's go deeper into this topic, because intimacy requires us to go to a deeper level.

To be intimate with someone means you are so comfortable being around this person that you expose your vulnerabilities and weaknesses. Intimacy requires a person to be open-minded. Your mate will reveal secrets to someone that haven't been revealed to another person. *Intimacy* requires trust. Additionally, intimacy can reveal one's weaknesses. What are some issues that you find hard to get over? What are some things in your life that you do repeatedly even though you know it does not feel right? *Vulnerability* refers to openness and honesty, whereas, *weakness* refers to lack of control or discipline. Vulnerability and weakness define real intimacy in a relationship. Without these two, there can be no intimacy in the relationship and the couple will have a difficult time staying together. The same reason God requires us to be intimate with Him is the same reason we need to be intimate with our significant other. Intimacy draws us closer to God, and draws us closer to our significant other.

Don't reveal your weaknesses or vulnerabilities until you have complete trust in the other person. Protect and guard your heart and don't reveal too much too soon. Only reveal a little bit of yourself at a time.

Here are a few scriptures that show us how intimacy allows us to connect with the other person. *Psalm 42:1* reads, *"As the deer pants for the water brooks, so pants my soul for You, O God."* To *pant* means to long eagerly for something like you are desperate for it. It also means to throb, labor or intensify your speed for something that you eagerly desire and seek, like how a deer pants for the water to quench his thirst or appetite. David, the author of the book of Psalms, compares his thirst for God like a deer thirsts for water. In other words, he is longing for intimacy with God because his soul needs replenishing and his thirst for God needs to be quenched. He is longing for a connection, bond and personal relationship with God. His soul yearns for the love of God, not anything physical or tangible. He asks God for His Holy Spirit to reside in him, make provision for him, and to renew his heart and mind. David is longing for spiritual intimacy.

James 4:8 reads, *"Draw near to God and He will draw near to you."* This scripture speaks in volumes, where we have a clearer understanding on the term *intimacy*. *To draw* means to attract, to pull towards you, to sway someone else towards your side, to allure someone else towards you and to cause someone to come in your direction. Therefore, God will draw us to him, but to get closer to Him or more intimate with Him, then we must pray, attend church regularly, meditate, fast, and read God's Word. All of these things require time and effort. Didn't we just talk about time and effort earlier?

Time and effort both develop intimacy. If a man is spending time with you such as talking to you on the phone, praying with you, taking you out on a dinner date, sending you texts and emails, and doing other affectionate and meaningful things to get to know you, then you will achieve the level of intimacy in your relationship. However, you must do it on a regular basis to stay connected to the person you have been drawn to. Once a person is drawn to you, it is harder for him to pull away because he is attracted to you. In other words, now that you have connected with this person, a bond is formed and it is harder for this bond to be broken. God is drawn to us because He cannot resist someone who is showing Him affection, attention, love, and admiration. In addition, God is drawn to someone who worships and praises Him. God does not turn away from anyone who is drawn to Him. He will draw to us and grant us the desires of our heart. Again, the same concept of intimacy with God applies in our relationships.

When we draw someone to us, this means a person propels the attraction and feels obligated to be in an intimate relationship. Intimacy forces you to keep digging, searching, and focusing until you have concluded that the person is "into you." This makes the relationship have a stronger bond, where you don't want out. Consequently, many relationships end because of irreconcilable differences and infidelity, which happen when there is a spiritual and emotional disconnect. In other words, there is a lack of communication. If you have difficulty relating to one another, resolving disputes and respecting each other, then that means that your "fire" (intimacy), has gone out in the relationship and needs to be rekindled.

A person who is drawn to you is least likely to leave you because there is a force within him that makes him stay. That force is called *intimacy*, which means he is "into me."

Keep in mind that a person experiences heartbreak only when he/she has established an emotional, spiritual, and physical connection with the other person. The person does not experience a broken-heart, sadness, or pain from a strictly sexual relationship because it was only physical. Like I said earlier, any two people can have sex without having any emotional attachment to the other person. To experience the heartache and pain, then you must have developed an intimate relationship. In other words, you have connected with him/her on all three levels. When the relationship fails, you are left vulnerable, where you feel hurt and sad. He/she has broken your heart because you gave him your love. Think about it for a moment and let this revelation ponder in your mind.

We need intimacy, not just a sexual encounter. Yes, sex can be good and enjoyable, but without a connection, it will not last. Eventually, you will want more than a "booty call" or a "one-night stand." Sex should not be a casual encounter where you go from one sexual partner to another sexual partner. It should be taken more seriously and there should be a long-term commitment established in your relationship before any sexual contact occurs. However, if you engage in such promiscuous behaviors, you are selling your body cheap. You are compromising your self-worth and value every time you "casually" engage in sex. In addition, you are losing "you" because a piece of you dies every time you give up your value in a meaningless manner. (I'll elaborate on this later in the book)

What is casual sex? *Casual sex* is having sex with someone for sexual pleasure. *Casual sex* is sex without recourse, meaning there is no commitment or desire to be in a relationship with the other person. In other words, you do not expect anything in return. You only want sex, and that's it. *Casual sex* is living with someone, whom you are not married to. Southern people call it "shacking up." Some people have lived under the same roof for several years without any long-term commitment such as marriage. For example, you have been living with the person for five years and you are no closer to marriage than when you started dating. This is what I call "a long-term girlfriend or boyfriend." You have no plans to get married and content with being someone's long-term partner. Actually, to be frank, this is what I call wasting valuable time. When a relationship is going nowhere, you are wasting your time and he is wasting yours. That's a whole lotta wasting time, isn't it? (I know I'm speaking Ebonics. Gotta keep it real.) Don't you have something better to do with your time than waste it on a dead-end relationship, like maybe working on your business plan or ministry function or whatever gift God has given you? Okay, let me tell you this. There was a couple who was engaged for twelve years. Are you kidding me? Ladies, what are you thinking? Ladies, I'm singling you out because it's your fault if you play yourself like that and play housewife for that long period of time and accept that type of treatment from a man. Well, I just said the key word "playing housewife". Bingo! That's it. That's the problem right there ladies. If you stop acting like you are married and uphold some standards and criteria, then he'll shape up and fly right. Hello somebody? Stop cooking, cleaning, doing the laundry and having sex with him and you'll see what his reaction will be. He'll either get himself together and put a ring on your finger or leave and find someone else to play house with. Stop settling ladies. You were created to be a wife, not a long term girlfriend, baby momma, his sidekick, or anything else other than a wife. Start operating in your God-given role.

> Reveal your standards upfront before a friendship develops. Refuse to be a casualty and let him know you're a commodity. You are wife material.

Therefore, when we desire a deeper, meaningful and valuable relationship, we need to get to know the person before sleeping with him. How do we get to know someone on an intimate level? Intimacy begins with developing a friendship first. We are so quick and in a hurry when we meet someone that we start dating immediately and begin telling others we are in a relationship. We never develop intimacy. When I hang out with my girlfriends, we laugh, cry, pray for each other, and even argue over who will treat when we go out. We enjoy making the other person happy. We also share our goals, aspirations, and dreams. We attend church together. Frequently, we will do things as a group to keep our connection and bond. We are available for each other. There are only a selected few young women that I allow in my inner circle besides my six sisters.

Is it possible to have the same type of friendship with a man as you do with your girlfriend? I believe so. *Proverbs 18:24* reads, *"A man who has friends must himself be friendly, but there is a friend who sticks closer than a brother."* The friend is Jesus Christ. Jesus will always be there. There are no limitations to His love and commitment to us. However, we have limitations and boundaries with our love. We have a difficult time expressing unconditional love because as humans we are caught up in the person's flaws,

13

imperfections, and failures. We fail to notice his potential and future possibilities. When we concentrate on the issues and not on the solutions, it will be difficult to be friends. To be friends, we have to accept the good and the bad.

A real friend loves you regardless, nonetheless, despite your flaws and imperfections. She loves you just because of who you are.

Based on my original statement, we can be friends with someone of the opposite sex. The same things that I share with my girlfriends, I would love to share with a young man. I would like us to be able to speak honestly and openly to one another, pray and encourage one another, and go out on dates. We can laugh and have fun and enjoy each other's company.

We should strive for a relationship without prerequisites or conditions. My friends and I enjoy each other's company and we don't expect anything in return. We are overjoyed to see each other, talk, laugh, share our intimate moments, and have fun. Don't you want to have these things with a man? If you do, they will not develop overnight. It takes time and patience to establish a friendship because you first have to lay the foundation, which is trust. I know you don't trust someone when you first meet that person, right? You have to build your friendship by spending time with him, sharing your goals and ideas, praying for one another, and being able to accept the person for the way he is. In other words, you allow the person to be himself, not trying to change him or mold him to your preferences, and that's where you can go wrong in the relationship. You think you can change him or mold him to be what you want him to be, but the only person who can change anyone is Jesus Christ.

Once you get it in your minds that you can't change him and realize you have to accept him the way he is at this very moment, then things will get a whole lot better for you. Either you like him right now, flaws and all or you don't. You will have to accept that what you see is really what you will get. Period! If you can accept what you see in him right now, then accept it. If you don't, then move on and don't try to change him to be what you won't him to be because you won't succeed. Yes, you can pray to God as God is the only one who can change anybody, but you may have to wait a long time for that change to take place. If you are willing to wait, go for it. I ain't madatcha! (I know I'm talking Ebonics. Gotta keep it real.) I've been waiting a long time for a husband, so I'm not willing to wait unnecessarily if I don't have to. He has to come ready-made for me like those Grand buttermilk biscuits you buy in the grocery store. Y'all know what I'm talking about. Just pop it open, the biscuits fall out and you just put those babies in the oven and wa la. They're ready to eat! Yummy! That's what I want: a man that's requires little to get ready. Ha, Ha. Okay, let's keep going. We got a lil ways to go. Are ya'll having fun and enjoying our conversation? I hope so.

My friends allow me to be myself and accept me the way I am. Sometimes, I can get on my friends' nerves or say hurtful things. They will tell me about it. We discuss it, resolve it, and move on. They will tell me when I am wrong and steer me in the right direction. Honest friends want to see you excel and prosper. They will offer godly counsel and advice when needed. They will be there for you when you call—period. *"As iron sharpens iron, so a man sharpens the countenance of his friend" (Proverbs 27:17).*

We are to establish a friendship first, and then a sincere relationship will follow. Once we are friends, we will be prepared for what comes next. There is a saying that good friends become great lovers. I believe this statement to be true; however, not all of our friends are our lovers. Some are meant to be platonic friends. You only see and value them as a friend. Be careful not to cross that boundary of your friendship, to have sex. A *platonic friendship* means there is no romantic connection or sexual contact. You are only friends and nothing more.

A friendship develops into a relationship and a relationship develops into marriage.

Consequently, you may both have a lot in common, where there is a physical attraction and you enjoy being in each other's company. You have been friends for quite some time, and then take it to the next level for something more serious and concrete. Do not jump in too quickly by dating and then deciding you just want to be friends. It is hard to become friends after a bad relationship. Why? Because you have allowed your emotions and feelings to get involved, and now you have revealed your vulnerabilities and weaknesses to someone else. As a result, you are hurt, disappointed, and heartbroken. In other words, you have established intimacy with the other person. It's hard to be friends with someone after he/she hurts you, which is why it is so important to establish a friendship first to connect with the person. Although the relationship may not last, chances are you can remain friends since you have established a solid foundation early on. Do not put your heart first, instead go head first. In other words, we are not to share everything and open up to a person immediately. We have to tap into his mind. Remember intimacy is all about getting "into his head" and then working our way "into his heart".

> Think with your head first, not your heart. That way, you will think cognitively and rationally and not be led by your emotions.

The best example of what real intimacy is all about is to examine two people in the Bible who were friends first before they were lovers. It is the story of God's creation of man and woman, which is found in the book of Genesis. Adam and Eve were naked in the garden. They did not know they were naked until they sinned by eating the forbidden fruit. There was no physical contact until after they sinned. After they sinned, their eyes were open and they knew they were naked and started covering themselves with fig leaves. *Genesis 2:25* reads, *"And they were both naked, the man and his wife, and were not ashamed."* This scripture indicates that emotional and spiritual connections were already established before sex took place. Adam and Eve were friends before they became lovers. In *Genesis 2:23*, Adam says woman is the bone of his bones and flesh of his flesh because she was taken from the rib in his side. Symbolically, they were joined as husband and wife before consummating the marriage. Do you see this? They were connected first without physical intimacy, which indicates that sex is not the dominating factor in the relationship.

> Sex does not equate to intimacy, but marriage does.

We placed so much emphasis on sex, but God views it as the least important factor. Sex came after Adam and Eve ate the forbidden fruit. They were already married. Earlier, the couple was enjoying each other's company, where they were open and honest with one another. They were comfortable with who they were. God, in His infinite wisdom, knew exactly what we needed because He placed a greater emphasis on establishing emotional and spiritual intimacy before sexual intimacy.

Before your birth, God knew exactly what you needed to function in this thing called "life." He knew exactly what would sustain our relationships. Guess what, it definitely isn't sex. We were wrong! We made a big deal about it and placed such an emphasis on sex that we overlooked the other areas in the relationship where we needed to focus our attention on. We believed that if we pleased our husbands or wives in the bedroom that everything will work out for the best. Our marriage will be okay. The wife believed that the husband would not commit adultery as long as she continued sleeping with him and meeting his physical needs. Well, guess what? He still left you for another woman, even after he had sex with you. This tells us that sex was not the cause of your breakdown, or his reason for committing adultery. There were other factors involved such as the lack of a spiritual and emotional connection.

God made sex as an added benefit. He created sex for humans to enjoy and receive pleasure, but after intimacy was established. I believe that Adam and Eve would have consummated the marriage even if they did not sin because they were joined together as husband and wife when God took the rib from Adam to create Eve. God created humans to have sexual desires. However, God was upset with Adam and Eve for not following directions. Because of their disobedience, he punished them. Their punishments were for Eve (woman) to have painful labor when she bore a child, and Adam (man) to till the ground and work for what he needed or wanted. Overall, the couple was able to have sex, enjoy it, but pain would follow. Therefore, the first marriage under covenant between Eve and Adam is what real intimacy is all about because they did not have sex before they were married. They were joined (married) first, and then had sex. Consequently, God forbids premarital sex.

Disobedience will bring about punishment from God.

We have been doing things backwards for far too long and it's time we start doing things the right way by refraining from any sexual contact until we get married. Doing it our way leads to fornication, adultery, pornography, and other sexual sins that pull us farther away from God. Sin separates us from God. Doing it God's way will lead to an enduring, fulfilling relationship with the person God ordained for us and will also draw us closer to God. Doing it God's way also means we stop searching and looking, but start waiting and planning. We start waiting on God's timing for our mate. We plan ahead for the marriage originally ordained by God. Marriage is more than a legal agreement. It is a covenant made by two people joining together to become as one, under God's govern or union. Again, a marriage needs intimacy, which is lacking in many marriages today and why people are finding a difficult time staying together.

Let's Stay Together with Intimacy

1. After reading the explanations on what real intimacy is about, can you honestly say that you established intimacy before having sex with the person you are with now? In other words, were you friends first before you became lovers? If you answered yes, can you distinguish the differences of whether he is a friend, lover, or only a platonic friendship? If you answered no, why did you have sex before establishing an intimate connection, which is establishing an emotional and spiritual connection? Did you have sex because of convenience, hormones on overload, obligation, or loneliness? Think about why you had sex.

2. In your own words, what does intimacy mean to you? In answering this question, think about those things that your spouse or significant other does or does not do and what you would like him to begin doing in your relationship. Additionally, think about the most intimate moment (besides sex as we discussed that sex really doesn't define intimacy) that was shared with your significant other and how it made you feel. If you had new opportunities to spend time with your mate, what are some things you would do while you are together?

3. What does sex really mean to you? How does sex make you feel? This is going to require you to reevaluate why you're having sex.

FIRST KEY TO ACHIEVE PHYSICAL INTIMACY IS PRAYER

It should come as no surprise that I would list prayer as the first key to achieve real physical intimacy. Did you think that foreplay only referred to body oils, rose petals, whip creams, and bubble bath? Most people believe that foreplay is what you read in Zane's *Sex Chronicles*, which focus entirely on the physical aspect of the relationship, which is sex. Conversely, I want to show you how to connect to the emotional and spiritual side of your being.

Did you know that foreplay is more mental than it is physical? First, relate to someone on a mental level, and then the physical attraction will fall in line. Women are emotional and sensitive human beings. Therefore, we are governed by what we hear. Men, on the other hand, are governed by what they see. Men are physical creatures, who observe a woman's physique and presence. The key to a woman's heart is to connect with her emotionally and spiritually. Once you can do that, the sexual intercourse will be intimate rather than just physical. You will begin to make love to your spouse and not have just another sexual experience.

Prayer is an essential ingredient in any relationship because it forms and strengthens the connection or bond with another person. There is no compromise if you desire a strong, solid relationship. Prayer is your lifeline to communicating with God. One must come humbly before God in prayer. In order to pray more fervently for the other person, you have to know the person that you are praying for. Prayer is a powerful tool that develops your character, ignites the humility inside of you, and makes you meek and strong at the same time. Prayer improves your self-worth and value. I want you to understand how important it is to connect with someone on a spiritual level. I heard a pastor say that we are more spiritual than we are human, because God is Spirit and we worship Him in spirit and in truth (See *John 4:24*).

Prayer sustains the relationship and creates a tighter bond that can't be easily broken.

We need prayer to sustain us in our everyday life. Prayer is our survival. Without prayer, we will have a difficult time operating in this world. Prayer draws us closer to God. As we get closer to God, we will be better, wiser, and stronger.

Here is a scripture that I believe will help you in your relationships. *Matthew 18: 20* reads, *"For where two or three are gathered together in my name, I am there in the midst of them."* There is power in unity. A bond cannot be broken easily when prayer is attached to it. God is saying in this scripture, whatever problems or situations arise, come together in prayer. *Coming together* means both of you have to humble yourselves before God and acknowledge that you are nothing without Him. If both of you agree that God is your lifeline and depend on Him to guide you, then God will hear your prayers and move on your behalf. Not only will He hear your prayer, He is in your midst. He promises to hear you, answer you, and be right there to help you get through whatever situation that you are going through. Wow! Thank you Jesus! When the two of you are having communication problems and your marriage is taking a downward spiral, then the both of you have to agree that you cannot work it out by yourselves. You need God to intervene on your behalf. All you have to do is acknowledge that you need God's help to sustain you. All God is doing is waiting for you to admit that you need Him. Once you come to that realization, He will help you get through it.

> There is *power* in unity.

Here is another scripture that talks about the importance of prayer. *1 Thessalonians 5:17* teaches you to pray without ceasing, meaning you must pray all the time, at any time, for any reason and pray for each other. *"Be anxious for nothing, but in everything by prayer and supplication, with thanksgiving, let your requests be known to God" (Philippians 4:6).* Every decision you make, you should not make it without God. If you have a difficult time committing as one, don't you think you will have an even harder time being as ONE when you unite in marriage? You have two different people with two different mentalities who have the difficult and challenging task in uniting as one. It would seem impossible to me to do that alone. You need some advice and counsel. You need someone who knows you inside and out to help you become ONE with your mate and what better person to assist you than the one who created you in the first place. Your marriage cannot survive on just the two of you. There is a high divorce rate in our society because we rely on our emotions and feelings so much that we make hasty, irrational decisions. Don't let your emotions lead you as if you do, then everything will start falling apart. Only when the both of you can come together and seek God, He will reveal things to you and show you things that will help improve your marriage so you can have a long-lasting marriage.

I would like to mention one more important scripture that outlines the importance of prayer. *James 5:16* reads, *"Confess your trespasses to one another, and pray for one another, that you may be healed. The effective, fervent prayer of a righteousness man avails much."* This scripture tells you that you have to repent and confess your faults to one another and then you must go to God in prayer. Once you are able to admit your wrongdoings, then God will hear your prayer and cleanse you from your sins. Confessing your wrongdoings is so important in having a healthy, strong relationship.

Many of you do not like to admit when you have made a mistake, so by confessing; you are able to humble yourselves and admit to your wrongdoing and ask for forgiveness. Being able to say "I'm sorry" is so important in a relationship because you have admitted to the other person that you made a mistake. In laymen's terms, you have taken responsibility for your actions. This is why a lot of our relationships are falling apart because no one wants to take ownership. It's easier to blame the other person rather than admit that you were the one that messed up. Playing the blame game will not solve anything and will not get you anywhere. In fact, it just makes everything worse because nothing gets accomplished and the both of you are in the same predicament when you began. When you begin to confess your faults, the door is open for forgiveness. This is a little something extra for you: pick your disagreements wisely as some things are not worth discussing.

Take responsibility for your actions because someone has to be the responsible person in order to resolve the conflict.

Another part to this scripture that many of you probably overlooked is the part about being righteous. You can go to God in prayer whether you are righteous, meaning holy, or not. In this case, if you are living righteous lives, this type of prayer avails much, meaning it is to your biggest advantage. It is a gain or benefit to you if you are living holy.

Do you see why prayer is essential in your relationships? Prayer is the key that holds things together. It unites you, makes you stronger, and better individuals and the best part about prayer is that it draws you closer to God. Again, you do not have to be saved to pray to God, since He hears all of your prayers. If you are living holy and righteous, your prayer is beneficial to you because God is inclined to answer your prayer.

A family that prays together will stay together. Therefore, as a couple continue to pray and seek God and watch God move in your marriage. Prayer is the authentic key to intimacy. When you pray as a couple, you will achieve real intimacy. Again, when you connect spiritually and mentally, your bond will be stronger. This is what foreplay is all about.

A family that prays together stays together.

Let's Stay Together with Prayer

1. What type of prayer life do you and your significant other possess? In other words, how often do you pray together? What things keep you from having an active prayer life? What changes will you begin making today that will make your prayer life stronger?

2. Think about all the times that you and your significant other pray. Who prays the most, you or your significant other? Also, do you pray for each other every time you pray together? Why or why not? What do you find yourselves praying about the most or the least and how will you change the focus of your prayers going forward?

3. In this chapter, I mentioned several Scriptures that outline the importance of prayer. *James 5:16* elaborates on confessing and praying for one another. Do you and your spouse have problems confessing your faults to one another? What keeps you from being completely open and honest with your spouse and admitting your mistakes? Is it pride, shame, guilt, or insensitivity? What are you doing about those issues that keep you from confessing and praying for one another and being open with one another so you can have a stronger prayer life and a greater level of intimacy in your relationship?

SECOND KEY TO ACHIEVE PHYSICAL INTIMACY IS PRAISE

The second key to achieving real physical intimacy in your relationship is to praise and uplift your significant other. These principles are basic principles. However, we have problems implementing these principles in our relationship. When you get into a relationship, it is no longer about you, as there is another person that you also have to consider. I know making that transition will be a little challenging for me after being alone for so long. God will have to work on me as I have become accustomed to the "I and me" motto. Once in a relationship, I have to make a new transition in my way of thinking.

To keep a relationship strong and healthy, you have to encourage and edify each other. Women have to be cheerleaders for our men because they need to hear what they are doing right and not hearing what they are doing wrong all the time. Everyone knows that praise lifts our spirits and prompts us to do better. It raises our self-esteem and our self-worth when we are told that we can do anything if we put our mind to it. Then, we will eventually start believing it. When we know that we have someone else in our corner that believes in us and values us, then we will begin to see that same value in ourselves.

Be a cheerleader for your mate because he needs you in his corner rooting for him. You are the one he spends the majority of his time with, so ensure he hears more cheering from you than ridicule and rejection.

Women like to hear good things because we are emotional and sensitive human beings. Men like to hear nice things about themselves too. It boosts their ego and makes them feel confident because they are doing the right thing and making you happy.

You need to praise, edify, and encourage your husband because he needs to know that you will stand beside him even when he loses a job. Will you still "ride or die" with him even when he has a terminal illness? Will you comfort and console him even when you know the decision he made was not the right one? Will you support his new business idea or tell him it's not worth the investment? You might even tell him that it is not the right time to get involved. Ladies, these qualities are what a man looks for in a woman. If you can dance with him in the rain and in the sunshine, you are a keeper and men need that.

In the book of Genesis, when Adam and Eve sinned in the garden, God removed man out of the garden because of his disobedience, but God didn't put Eve out. *"Therefore the Lord God sent **him** out of the garden of Eden to till the ground from which he was taken. So he drove out **the man**; and He placed cherubim at the east of the garden of Eden, and a flaming sword which turned every way, to guard the way to the tree of life" (Genesis 3:23-24).* The scripture reads that God put him out of the garden, not them, and drove out "the man," meaning a particular person, a single individual. The word "the" acts as an adjective that describes the noun "man," meaning one person. Therefore, God put Adam out, not Eve because God gave the instructions to Adam and not Eve. God also addressed Adam about the decision he had made and didn't say one single thing to Eve. God put Adam in charge, and when he fell, they both were punished because they were joined together as one and God acknowledged them as one. Eve was already Adam's wife when he fell and she stood by her man. He got in trouble and she hung in there with him. She did what she was supposed to do without anyone giving her the book, *How to Be a Wife for Dummies*. Loyalty and commitment is in a woman's makeup. This is our natural behavior. We have it in us if we tap into what God already placed in us as a wife.

God told the man to leave, but of course, they were joined together as husband and wife, so Eve went with her husband. Remember, a husband and a wife is joined together as one, meaning they operate in unity. What happens to one affects the other. I know most of you have never read this scripture or heard it explained in this way, but the revelation I got is that God wants to teach us the importance of staying together and what being as "one" really means. Adam blamed his wife instead of taking responsibility for his actions. In that one instance, he responded as a follower and not as the leader that God called him to be. Men, know your role as head of the household and be mindful of the decisions you make as they affect not just you, but those around you.

> Women are to stand by their men and support them through the good and bad times.

How does praising someone else lead to physical intimacy? There is an old saying that states "the key to a man's heart is through his stomach." This is a myth because men in today's society can "throw down" in the kitchen and still be nonchalant and emotionally unattached in a relationship. I believe that the key to a man's heart is through his ears, just like for the woman. Yes, men are enticed with how a woman looks, but it's what you say to him that will get into his heart and keep it. How the woman looks attracts him physically, but what you say and how you say it attract him spiritually and emotionally and those two things are what makes them leaders and providers. A man cares a lot about how a woman looks and the woman may get his attention based on her physical appearance, but it is highly unlikely she will gain access to his heart if that is all she has to offer. Even if the sex is good, if all a man hears from his woman is nagging about what he isn't doing, should be doing, how horrible he is and all types of negative and degrading things, he will eventually leave.

Degrading a man is the worst thing you can do to him because it insults his manhood and his authority and position of being a leader and provider. He will leave you for someone else who will praise him, even if the sexual intercourse is not that great. Gentleman, am I right? For a man, all he cares about is having sex and he doesn't really care if it's good sex or bad sex because sex is a release for him. All he wants to do is release himself. For a woman, she can tell good sex from bad sex because she receives what the man releases into her. A woman can tell if what she receives is good, meaning she likes it or it is bad, meaning she doesn't like it. A man releases (outputs) into the woman and she receives his inputs. That's why women have to be careful and selective about what is being imparted inside of them from a man and I'm not talking about semen. (Thanks to a dear friend who brought this up to me). Okay y'all, let's really talk about this.

Women need to be concerned now with far more things other than pregnancy and STD's. Not only is your physical well-being at stake, but also your spiritual

30

and emotional well-being. I'm talking about attitudes, emotions, spiritual attachments, different spirits such as envy, strife, lust, pride, jealousy, mental incompetence, etc. To break it down further, I'm talking about everything the man possesses inside of him will be imparted inside of you. You were made from man; therefore, you were designed to have some of the man's qualities in you. (Remember, woman was made from a rib that came out of the man). The key is that you have to connect to the right man (rib) to obtain the good qualities that he possesses. Now, think about these things real hard ladies the next time you want to sleep with a man who is not the husband that God ordained for you.

Let's go deeper into this as I wanna make sure you know how valuable sex is. Have you noticed subtle to drastic changes in a woman after she gets into a new relationship? Before she hooked up with him, she was outgoing, fun, nice, sweet, caring and an all around girl. Now, she's cold, always upset and got an attitude and don't even have time for you as she once did. She did a 360. Those are clear signs of a problematic relationship. I know you ladies know what I'm talking about as I'm probably talking about you. Ouch! Remember ladies, the man imparts into you. What's in him will be deposited into you. So, don't you dare fool yourself to believe those lies you tell yourself that "it's just sex" or "it didn't mean anything". With him, it may have been just sex, but because you received from him, you will get what he dished out. Be very selective of who you sleep with as you are receiving more than just sex. Sex for women affects us in many different ways and one of those ways is emotionally. We either change for the good or the bad depending on the internal characteristics of the man. Ladies, I am spending quite a bit of time describing in detail about impartation from the man because it is extremely important that you take this in consideration. What are you receiving from him? Please think about these things ladies. Remember ladies, Eve received a piece of Adam. She received a rib from him and once they were joined sexually, she received far more than a physical piece, but also emotional and spiritual attachments. Okay, let's move on. I think you got it.

Now, let's get back to talking about praise. For a woman, she will look past a man's looks and totally concentrate on what he is saying to her. A man knows what to say to a woman in order to sleep with her. He plays on her emotions and feelings by giving her compliments on the things she wants to hear. If a man can connect to a woman's emotions, then the emotional connection will lead to a sexual relationship. I am not saying that all a man has to do is to say kind words to a woman and she will sleep with him. Not every woman is gullible, since there are many who value themselves. What I'm saying is that the key to a woman's heart is through her ears and is also true for the man as well. Both are enticed with words. Praises and compliments work on both sexes. Couples desire to have a healthy and fulfilled marriage.

Jesus loves when we praise and worship him. As a matter of fact, he requires it because the Bible states that if we don't praise him, then rocks will. We are made in his likeness and image, so it is in our natural scope that we love praise as well. It helps our inner confidence.

I want to share with you a real life situation that exemplifies how praise works. The names are changed to protect their identities. Susan was in a new relationship with Paul. She had known Paul for a few months. She believed she was in a serious relationship with him. They did not establish a friendship because on their first date, they kissed. Some feel it is okay to kiss on the first date. However, I was shocked and upset because I am thinking, 'you kissed someone you don't even know yet.' Why? For those of you who read my first book, *The Seven Deadly Sexual Sins*, I explain the importance of kissing between couples. I do not take this topic lightly. I also do not believe in engaging in casual sex.

On their second date, Paul promised to marry her because he loved her and wanted her to be his forever. He also promised her that he would cherish and provide for her. He spoke all these wonderful things to fill her head. Ladies, you know we all like to hear those things. This was music to her ears and she fell for him abruptly. This is what praise will do to a woman. Their relationship was on good terms until he had to travel out of town to care for his sick mother. Once he left town, their communication decreased. She was calling and texting him constantly and he did not respond back. She also asked me to call him for her to see what was going on. I did not because chasing after a man shows a sign of desperation. There were some misunderstandings and communication problems in the relationship. I am not sure of the outcome of the relationship or if the relationship worked out or not. However, when we go in with our hearts without using our heads, it can be disastrous. We can open our hearts to him once we have established a solid foundation, which as I stated earlier, begins with establishing a friendship. If the relationship becomes serious where a commitment is made, then we know we have someone who we can spend the rest of our lives with.

Hopefully, this example explains what I am saying. Women are governed by what we hear. Keep in mind that we are emotional and sensitive creatures. We long for praises and compliments. We like to be nurtured and have someone provide for our welfare. When we hear these pleasant words, men can have us in their pocket and have us believing that they are "into us," when they really aren't. We have to stop looking for attention in all the wrong people. It makes us look desperate and foolish and that's not attractive at all. Take the time to see if he's really sincere and genuine as you will clearly tell by his actions. Trust me ladies. If he can't back up his talk, then you need to walk him right out of your life. Some men just ain't worth it. Ladies, we have to stop rushing into these relationships and take our time. If he's sent by God, he won't go anywhere and if he ain't sent by God, then he'll find the next woman to try to play over.

Ladies, I want to share something with you that I put on Facebook that I believe will help you in your dating relationships. You need to give the **next** man who has the potential of being **your** man three tests to see if he is worthy of being your man. The first test you should give him is a credit check. You need to check his background to see if he has a relationship with God. Check his prayer life, his knowledge of God's word, church attendance, tithing beliefs, fasting habits and so forth. Check him out. The second test you need to give him is a blood test as you want to ensure he is covered by the blood of Jesus, meaning he has accepted Jesus Christ into his life. Lastly, you need to give him a criminal background check to make sure he's not running from God, which means he's not running away from his purpose or destiny. If he fails either one of these tests, then he is not the right one for you. If you don't care about any of these things, then you can go out and date any man you want. But, for those of us who know our worth and value and have a relationship with Jesus Christ, then we should administer all of these tests during the friendship stage. You need to find out early on what type of man he is and whether he is the right one for you. I guarantee you that you will weed out a whole lot of "be's" out of your life. For example, wanna be (He wanna be your man), could be, (he could be your man) and should be (he should be your man).

Ladies, we should also refrain from revealing our weaknesses and vulnerabilities too quickly in a relationship because men can take advantage of us, which is why we should go into a new relationship with our heads, instead of our hearts. Don't talk too much, too soon. Let him in gradually until you know he is trustworthy. Also ladies, let him do a lot of the talking and listen intensely to what he is saying. You'll find out a lot about him without him realizing that you're checking him out. He'll either shoot himself in the foot and have you ready to skip dessert and we can't have that as dessert is the part of the meal that women look forward to, (I know I do) or have you dreaming about yall's wedding day. Lol. I hope it's the latter.

> Guard your heart and let him in gradually, a little bit at a time, until the relationship is solid enough that you are comfortable opening up to him.

Let's Stay Together with Praise

1. What type of things do you do or say to your significant other or spouse to praise him? How often do you express your true feelings or give your mate praise? If you rarely express your love to your spouse to uplift or encourage him, then what keeps you from doing or saying those things? What are some things you can do to improve your praise actions on a regular basis?

2. How do you feel when someone else praises or uplifts you? How do you feel when someone fails to praise or uplift you? Now, would you rather be the one who is praised or the one who is doing the praising? Does the relationship need both?

3. Discuss with your spouse or significant other things that he/she is doing that is praiseworthy or deserving of compliments. After the discussion with your mate, how does it make you feel and makes him feel afterwards? Were you taking him for granted by not praising him?

THIRD KEY TO ACHIEVE PHYSICAL INTIMACY IS PLAN AND PREPARATION

The third key to achieving real physical intimacy is to find a man with a plan. Ladies, I know you can back me up on this one, when I say that we like a man that has a plan. In other words, he has insight, vision, and direction for his life. If the man doesn't have a plan for his life, then he will not know where he is headed. A plan can be short-term or long-term. It can be choosing to spend the rest of your life with a certain person. A man could be planning a business venture to own his establishment within five years. He creates a business plan, reviews his finances (portfolio), and reviews what is needed to get his business started. Suppose, this man meets a pleasant and mature Christian woman whose background and experience is in investments or business. She is well-educated on how to handle finances and has the resources to get a business plan off the ground. Would an intelligent, Christian woman invest her time or resources into a relationship with this particular man? More than likely, she would. But what about the man who talks often of what he wants to accomplish and to own and never takes any action? What about the man who boasts about his goals and plans but has not shown initiative or any productivity towards bringing his goals or plans into fruition? Do you think an intelligent, Christian woman is going to invest her time or resources in his "talking without action" ideas? Of course, she won't. As the saying goes, talk is cheap. If you do not have your plan written down, you must not be serious about your vision. Write the vision and make it plain. *Habakkuk 2:1* reads, *"Write the vision and make it plain on tablets, that he may run who reads it. For the vision is yet for an appointed time."* Why? If you do not write your vision, how can you envision and see it coming to pass? Writing it down gives you something to look forward to and use as a guide to work towards your goal.

Write the *vision* and make it plain.

I watched Tyler Perry's movie entitled *A Family that Preys*. I want to highlight a few points from the movie. Perry's character and his best friend are construction workers. His character is a man who has no vision or purpose. He stopped dreaming and believing. However, Perry's friend is a man with a plan. He already had his business plan written up, where we see he had the vision, but lacked the means to carry it out. The reason I know that he wrote down his vision because he took his business plan to the bank in hopes of getting a loan to cover the expenses. Next, he asks his wife's boss for the startup money and he knew exactly how much he needed to get started. His vision is to have his own construction company. However, his wife played by the actress, Sanaa Lathan, only focuses on her own affairs and fails to recognize his true potential, and she does absolutely nothing to support him. Instead, she belittles him and puts him down, but her husband refuses to give up. He knows he has the knowledge and skills to make it happen, but what he does not have are the resources. In the end, his vision comes to pass because he does not let go of it. It appears rough in the beginning as if it is not going to happen after several banks turned him down for a loan. However, he still did not let go of his dream. The irony of the story is that through it all, he supports and helps his wife, who did not believe in him and was very unsupportive. There's way more to this story than what I am telling you. Moreover, I want you to see how important it is for a man to have a plan, to stick with his plan, and it is equally important that the wife support his vision and do whatever she can to see it into fruition.

What is the responsibility of the wife? How important is it for the wife to support her husband's vision? In answering these questions, I want to direct your attention to the woman in *Proverbs 31*, who was a modern-day woman or should I say wife as she was married. This type of wife, the Bible refers to as rare and priceless. This means you cannot put a price tag or a value on her. *Proverbs 31:10* reads, *"Who can find a virtuous woman? For her price is far above rubies."* A wife who can take care of the household, community, and makes wise business and investment decisions is what this scripture calls a *virtuous woman*. Many people who read this scripture assume that a "virtuous woman" is a woman who is a virgin; this is not possible since the woman was married. This wife took care of the children, maintained the house by cooking and cleaning, and still made sure her husband's needs were met. Besides this, the Bible states that she was an investor too, meaning she invested in real estate. It's important to note that before she invested in anything, she prayed about it. It reads, *"She considers the field, and buyeth it"* *(Proverbs 31:16)*. In other words, she used her resources wisely and not frivolously or wastefully. She worked outside the home as an entrepreneur who sold clothes, so she too helped bring in revenue inside the home. She also volunteered in her community by donating her time and resources to the poor and needy. She did it all with strength, confidence, and her faith in God.

> A *virtuous woman* is simply a "do-it-all-wife" who does everything with class, dignity, integrity, grace, humility, and love. She knows how to hold it down and she knows how to represent her man. She has it going on.

The Bible adds that her children were blessed and her husband praised all the things she did. This is the modern-day wife that a husband needs. This is how a wife helps her husband in doing his job and serves him best by offering her time, resources, support, encouragement, and gives spiritual advice to him. How important is the wife to the husband? A wife is extremely important to the husband because he would not be who God has called him to be without the support of his wife. Therefore, a wife is her husband's helper or backbone. Moreover, she is present in his life to hold him down and help him bring his dream into fruition. We will elaborate more on the wife's roles as a helpmeet to her husband later on in this book.

A man with a plan is icing on the cake for a woman. A woman likes a thinker and a man of action. Women like men who are go-getters and persistent in achieving their plans. Some men think that women need a plan too. But men need a plan more than women do because they are the ones God put in charge to have dominion over the earth. Men are the leaders and the head of the household. Men have the authority that God gave them to have dominion over the earth, whereas women are to be submissive to the men. *"Then God*

40

said, 'Let us make man in our image, according to Our likeness; let them have dominion over the fish of the sea, over the birds of the air, and over the cattle, over all the earth and over every creeping thing that creeps on the earth'" (Genesis 1:26).

When I say submit, I am talking about humility and meekness. This does not mean that the man can tell the woman what she can or cannot do, and to speak to her as a child. A man still has to respect the woman, cherish her, and treat her like the *queen* that she is. In return, the woman should treat him like the *king* that he is. Why doesn't a woman want to take care of her man when he is treating her like a queen? In most cases, it is not women that are mistreating the men. Men are mistreating and disrespecting women.

So not only do you have to plan, you also have to be prepared. You need to prepare for what comes next. In other words, prepare for the future. Some people say that you need to prepare for the worst. If something unexpectedly happens such as a loss of a job, are you prepared financially to still be able to meet the needs of the family? Financial analysts recommend we save 40% of our monthly income and to have at least six months of rent or mortgage payments in the bank. A financial breakdown is to take 10% of your income for tithes and/or offerings, 40% in savings, and pay bills on 60% of your income. Are we doing that right now? I know we all need to work on preparation, including myself, because we just do not know what will happen in the future. Yes, God will supply our needs and take care of us. We also have to do our part by using the wisdom God has given us to make wise and sound decisions with our money. In other words, ladies, we can't go shopping whenever we have a bad day or feel like spending money. Even if you have millions of dollars, you can still go broke. There are a whole lotta broke millionaires right now who probably ponder a whole lot on their past mistakes and what they used to have. I'm sure they have a lot of regrets and if they had a chance to do things over, they would. Unfortunately, what's done is done. We can learn from our mistakes and do our best not to repeat them, but we can't un-do.

> Saving shows that you're appreciative of what you have and that you value your future.

Aside from saving and investing, are you prepared to be a wife? The highlight of my single women's ministry is based on one scripture which is *Proverbs 18:22, "He who finds a wife finds a good thing, and obtains favor from the Lord."* We have quoted this scripture so many times, but ladies; do we honestly know what it really means? God has dealt with me a lot on this passage. Here are a few things I want to share with you that God showed me. First, he must find you, so you need to stop looking for him. Stop looking for him on the dating internet sites, in the clubs, or asking your friends to hook you up. Now, there's nothing wrong with a friend suggesting someone to you that she may think would be a great friend for you, but just because she may think he is right for you doesn't mean that he is. He could be the right one or he could be the wrong one. No one knows you better than you. Well, except God and he's got excellent taste and he doesn't miss the mark either. Best of all, He knows what you like and what you need and He'll bring someone to you that can give you both. There's only one catch: you gotta wait on Him. It's not as simple as it sounds, but not only is God worth waiting for, but also the man that

He brings to you will be worth waiting for as well. It's a win, win situation.

Second, he must find you as a wife, meaning you are prepared to be a wife when he finds you. How can I be a wife if I have never been married? Good question. The answer is this: there is no way to be prepared as a wife as we cannot prepare for salvation. If we could get ourselves ready and present ourselves faultless before God, there would be no need for salvation. To go even further, Jesus' dying on the cross for our sins would be in vain if we could prepare ourselves for living a holy righteous life. The Bible states that there is nothing we can do to get ourselves ready before Christ. We have to come just as we are so we can allow God to do His perfect work in us. This is the same as preparing to be a wife. A woman cannot prepare, but she can be ready to receive the husband that God sends to her. There is really no way to prepare to be a wife for the very first time. Most things you have to learn on your own. Am I right married couples? Even with all the marriage counseling, training and workshops the world provides to you, you will still mess up, have disagreements, and still at times feel like walking away, but through a whole lot of praying, you learn how to long-suffer with your mate. You won't get everything right, even with preparation, so I advise to get ready to receive him when God sends him. *2 Timothy 4:2 states "be ready in season and out of season. Convince, rebuke, exhort, with all longsuffering and teaching."* I believe it is more important to be ready than to be prepared. *Being ready* means to be on guard, be alert, in position and in the place where God wants you to be. Being ready means it will be easier finding you because you are in a position to be found. Get yourself ready and let God do his perfect work in you.

Listen ladies, you already have what it takes inside you to be a wife: cooking, cleaning, praying for someone else, caring for someone else, being responsible, considerate, kind, generous, loving, responsible, nurturing etc. These are some things a woman already possesses inside her to help her be ready before becoming a man's wife. A woman was born to be a wife. (See Genesis 2) Maybe she cannot prepare for everything, but she can use everything God has created her to be. Consider this: a woman who gives birth to a child for the first time has all the natural instincts inside her to properly care and meet the needs of her baby. Without having any baby momma training, she knows what to do and it amazes me what instincts a mother has that I don't even have because I'm not a mother. She knows when the baby is hungry, when he needs changing, why he is crying, when he needs to be held and nurtured, when he is sleepy, when he is agitated, when he is in pain or hurting, when he is sick, etc. She knows these things about her child without having ever babysat another child or having her own. Why? God put inside the woman nurturing instincts to care for others. It's a natural instinct. Ladies, what you need is already inside of you. Use the gifts you were born with. *James 1: 17 states "every good gift and every perfect gift is from above, and comes down from the Father of lights, with whom there is no variation or shadow of turning."* God freely gave us so many gifts that we haven't even tapped into yet. We were born gifted. Glory to God! He gave us gifts that we didn't even ask for nor did we qualify to receive them. In order words, we didn't do anything to receive these gifts. Let me show you how gifted you really are. It's a gift that a mother can properly care for a baby for the first time without ever having one. It's a gift when you can do something that

44

you've never done or never been taught how to do and do it well. It's a gift when you can offer someone sound advice and counsel on something you've never experienced or have knowledge in. It's a gift when we can love people who don't love us back and who treat us like dirt. Okay, I'm stretching this one, but don't we consider Jesus Christ a gift to us and since Jesus is love, then I believe loving is a gift, right? My point is that we have the gifts. What we have to do is protect our gifts from those who will misuse them or abuse them and use our gifts for the glory of God.

> You can't prepare to be a wife, but you can be ready to receive him when God sends him to you.

God did not prepare Eve to be Adam's wife. She came ready-made for him. She was formed out of Adam's rib, meaning she was made specifically for the man. This means that woman was made for the husband that God has for her. All she has to do is accept what God has already placed in her to be his wife. He has already given woman three things (gifts) that she needs to meet the needs of her husband. Eve had all these tools when she was formed from Adam's rib. No one prepared her for being a wife. She only had to tap into the gifts that God had already given her. Let us talk briefly about the three tools a woman already possesses to be a wife.

The first tool Eve possessed as a wife was a *spiritual connection* with God. When Adam and Eve sinned after eating the forbidden fruit, they hid themselves from the presence of God because they were convicted of their sin. In other words, they had a spiritual connection and relationship with the Father.

When they sinned, they were ashamed for what they had done. *Genesis 3:8* reads, *"And they heard the sound of the Lord God walking in the garden in the cool of the day, and Adam and his wife hid themselves from the presence of the Lord God among the trees of the garden."* If Adam and Eve did not fear and reverence God, then they wouldn't have hidden themselves. They felt guilty and ashamed because of their sin, so they hid themselves after hearing God, not actually seeing Him. They had an intimate relationship with God because they recognized His sound. Eve had a spiritual connection with God, which is the main ingredient in a relationship if it is going to be long-lasting. God has to be the head of your marriage.

Second, Eve was an emotional and nurturing human being. This is found in *Genesis 2:25, "And they were both naked, the man and his wife, and were not ashamed."* I want to explain what naked truly means. *Naked* means bare, exposed, uncovered, unhidden, revealed, and unashamed. They had an *emotional connection* since they were both naked and exposed, meaning they were comfortable with each other and had open, honest communication. They were also completely forward with one another to reveal their nakedness without embarrassment or humiliation. The Scripture states that they were unashamed. *Being a wife* means you have to expose your vulnerabilities and your weaknesses and Eve did that without anyone telling her how to do it.

The main sign to know you are ready to marry is when you are comfortable being completely naked in front of your mate and I don't mean in the physical sense.

Finally, the last tool that Eve possessed was the *physical* aspect of being a wife. God told Eve that her punishment for eating the forbidden fruit was painful labor. God blessed Eve to be fruitful and to multiply, which means to have sexual intercourse with her husband and conceive children. Therefore, God gave the gift of sex to Eve without anyone preparing her for it. God had already placed sexual desires in her. God made sex as a beautiful, wonderful experience for husbands and wives. They are to enjoy sex. Childbirth can produce painful labor and this is the punishment. Thankfully, God didn't take away sex; he only made bearing children difficult.

God gave women the emotional, spiritual, and physical tools that we need to be wives. All we have to do is use what God has already given us and be ready and open to receive the blessing when God sends him to us.

Finally ladies, you have to know that when he finds you, you are the "good thing" in his life. You have to know and believe that you are the one he is chasing after. In other words, you are what he has been looking for and God will bless that union. There is more than the man finding you as mentioned in the previous scripture. He is not looking for a mistress, baby momma, some chick-on-the-side, a one-night stand, or a long-term girlfriend. He has to find a wife. Now, the question you have to ask yourself is this: Do you believe you are wife material? If you believe it, then start living like it and stop settling for anything less and stop compromising your value for "a man" when what God wants to send you is "your man".

We know prayer, praise, and plan and preparation develop physical intimacy and women are completely turned on by these things. We need a husband to connect with us on the emotional and spiritual side in order to achieve a long-lasting, healthy, and fulfilling relationship. Notice, I say husband and not boyfriend or baby daddy because you need to be married first to fully receive the benefits of what I am telling you. It pleases God when we are obedient to His Word and when we please God, He will give us the desires of our heart.

We still have seven keys left. This is good stuff people. Ladies, I hope you are enjoying our conversation and taking everything in and answering the thought-provoking questions at the end of each chapter. They are designed to help you think and use wisdom. Gentlemen, I am helping you too whether you know it or not. You need to know what we want so you can snag a good wife. Remember, your favor comes from finding your wife, so I'm helping you find your favor. (See Proverbs 18:22) Married couples, I know the chapter on prayer helped you look at praying with your mate in a totally different light. You should also answer the thought-provoking questions at the end of the chapters as well. I hope all of you are being enlightened and beginning to take on a different perspective in your relationships.

Let's Stay Together with Planning and Preparation

1. What are your short-term and long-term goals? Do you have a plan to achieve those goals? Have you written out your plan? What is stopping you from achieving the plans you have laid out for your future?

2. How important is it to have a man who has a plan for his life? If it is important to you, then why aren't you doing anything about it? Did you settle for a man with no direction, purpose, or plan for his life? What would you do if you discovered that he has no intentions of marrying you or being in a committed relationship?

3. In this chapter on planning and preparation, I talked about planning financially for the future. Do you and your spouse have a budget? Do you and your spouse have a savings or investment account? What are you going to do today to change the financial course of your relationship to increase your savings or investment accounts?

FOURTH KEY TO ACHIEVE PHYSICAL INTIMACY IS PERFORMANCE

The fourth key to achieve real physical intimacy is performance. Wait a minute, ladies! Don't get too excited and start jumping up and down and giving each other a high-five. I can imagine you ladies going crazy right about now. I can also imagine hearing you say, "Tell him, sister!" "You're right on it, girl!" "You read our minds!" "He needs to know how to perform in the bedroom!" Yes, you are exactly right ladies. Physical intimacy is very important in a relationship, but what I feel that is missing in many relationships are an emotional and spiritual connection because if we can connect on those two levels, then the physical intimacy will be all the more special and enjoyable. We will keep our minds off our flesh and concentrate more on establishing a strong mental and spiritual connection, which is what this book is entirely about. So, bring it down a notch and let's keep our focus. Come on ladies. Stay focused. Remember, this book is not about sex per se. We are just talking around it. Get it?

In speaking about performance, I am talking about what type of character and personality the man has. In other words, does chivalry and romance still exist? Does he open the door for you, pull out your chair at dinner, and wait for you to be seated first before he sits down? Does he come up with suggestions and ideas for dates or does he wait for you to plan everything? Does he have spunk and swagger about him? Is he creative and spontaneous? Is he a fun and outgoing person, who likes to have fun and do exciting things? These are some of the things that I definitely look for in a man whom I am interested in dating. There are a few qualities you can see in a man that he will perform on a long-term basis. No one is perfect and every man does not have chivalric qualities or characteristics. However, every Christian man should know how to take care of his queen. Men, who were raised on the streets or in a violent, dysfunctional household, may not possess these qualities on how to treat a lady since they have never seen or experienced them. If all you ever see in the home is chaos, violence and confusion, then more than likely, that is what you will grow up imitating.

Ladies, hear me clearly, when I say that if you want a man to treat you like the queen that you are, you have to show and tell him how you want to be treated upfront. Steve Harvey hit it on the nail when he talked about these things in his book, *Act like a Lady, Think like a Man*. He states that women have to set the guidelines upfront on how we want our men to treat us and take care of us as some men just don't know how. It is not that they don't want to do it, some men do not know how and we have to tell them what we want and expect in the beginning of courtship.

Remember, dating comes after establishing a friendship, where you are comfortable sharing and conversing with each other. Give it about two or three dates and watch him as you take mental notes on what he does or doesn't do. This will show you what type of man he is. After the third date, tell him what you like for him to do. If he doesn't automatically open your door, pull out your chair, don't pay for the dinner, then tell him what you expect from him and do it sooner rather than later. Again, you determine when the right time to tell him what you expect of him without an attitude. If he doesn't do it, you know what type of man he is. If he listens to you, cares about you and desires for you to be in his life, he will do those things and even more because he respects and values you.

Actually, instead of telling him, I believe showing him is more effective. Don't get in the car if he doesn't open the door for you and don't sit down at the table if he doesn't pull out your chair. And ladies, definitely don't offer to pay for the dinner. Remember, you were paying for your own dinner before you started dating so he should add to you and not subtract from you. If you still have to pay in a relationship, then might as well as be alone and pay for your own self. Hello? Girlfriend, don't you dare sit down if he doesn't do the things I just mentioned. Hopefully, he will get the hint or be embarrassed at the dinner table if he is sitting down and you are still standing. A man knows a good woman when he sees one. He will do whatever he can to keep you. If he doesn't, he is not the right one for you. Don't waste your time and energy on something that just will not work.

> If chivalry still exists, you will see it in the person you are dating.

Not only is a man to perform for his woman, but also for her children. There are many single mothers who are reading this book and have ignored the warning signs. You have been concentrating so much on your happiness that you forgot about your child's happiness. Don't you want the man who is treating you with respect to also do the same thing for your child? Don't look at your child as being insignificant in your relationship.

Some women believe that if they are happy then the child(ren) will be happy too. This is not necessarily true since it depends on how you define happiness. If you define happiness as material possessions such as money, gifts, massages, pedicures, shopping trips, etc., but you ignore that he yells at you, disrespects you, cheats on you, and takes you for granted, then this is not happiness. That's not a healthy relationship because none of your emotional and spiritual needs are being met. Moreover, it will wreak havoc on your child if you do not establish these two things. It is not that you don't love your child. If you have been a single parent for a long time, you may settle for anyone offering to take care of you financially. Your bills are paid, but you are miserable on the inside and your child is feeling displaced and neglected.

Be mindful of who you date and how he performs for not only you, but your child as well. Let him know that if he wants you, he has to want your child. You come as a package deal. He cannot have one without the other. Some men only want you and not your child. Men don't want the responsibility of taking care of someone else's child, so you have to let them know what you stand for and what you represent. Don't settle for anything less than God's best. If you have to wait a little longer for the right man to come along, wait. It will be worth it in the end because God will send you a respectable and honorable Christian man who values you and will do anything he can to be with you, even establishing a relationship with your child too.

If you have children, make sure he knows that they come with courting you. No exceptions and no compromise. Make sure he knows this right away.

Men, all of these principles and concepts are what we want from you. Women need to know what qualities and characteristics to look for in a man and what defines real intimacy. Steve Harvey shared his views from a man's perspective in his book, *Act like a Lady, Think like a Man*. Since I am a woman, I have to speak from a woman's perspective and God has brought these issues to my attention concerning what is lacking in our relationships. There is way too much casual sex going on and we jump from one sexual partner to another sexual partner. We are seeking something that we haven't been able to put a finger on. We know something is missing, but cannot figure out what is missing. Some of you know what is missing in your relationship, but you ignore that missing piece because you have some internal conflicts-low self-esteem, loneliness, and depression—that you haven't dealt with yet. Consequently, you turn to sex to cover those issues. I highly recommend you purchase my first book, *The Seven Deadly Sexual Sins,* because it will help you deal with those issues.

When we start looking for love and affection in all the wrong places, we start being careless with our bodies by having sex with someone whom we know is not what we need. We do it anyway because it feels good temporarily. When the sex is over, you are still feeling empty and alone.

These simple principles will help you in developing a long-lasting, healthy relationship. The main ingredient that has been missing is the lack of intimacy. My hope and prayer is that if you take the time and effort in establishing the foundation first, which is friendship, that you will approach your relationships differently and take the time to know someone first before any physical contact ever occurs. I believe if you do this, you will not have to sleep around trying to find what you are looking for. I hope you will wait until marriage before you have sex because you need to know what type of man you're getting with. I know for many of you, this is somewhat difficult to do, but honestly, this is what God requires of us. *Romans 12:1* reads, *"I beseech you therefore, brethren, by the mercies of God, that you present your bodies a living sacrifice, holy, acceptable to God, which is your reasonable service."* What God requires of us is not beyond reason or capability. We have it in us to live holy if we make the choice to. We have to be obedient to His Word to live holy as our righteous living ensures us that we will get all the blessings that God has for us and I don't know about ya'll, but I want every single blessing that God has for me. I'll take yours too if ya'll don't want them. We have to establish boundaries and guidelines for ourselves while in courtship. We have to set the tone for the men because they will follow if we lead by example. I would like to add that we have to follow our own rules that we set. If we follow them, then they will follow them. We break and bend the rules that we set and that's when we fall into temptation. We tell him he has to leave at 10:00pm, but then we allow him to stay another hour and he will keep testing us and pushing us until we throw all of our rules out the window and just allow things to happen. It all starts with breaking one thing that we think is insignificant until we realize that all the criteria we set for ourselves, we no longer honor. The rules we set are more for our benefit than it is theirs. Think about it. Ya'll know I'm right.

> The rules and boundaries we set are more for our benefit than it is the person we are dating. They help us stay committed and disciplined to establishing a godly relationship.

Let's Stay Together with Performance

1. What chivalric things would you like to see from your mate that is important to you, but he's not currently doing? Did you establish early in the courtship what things you expect from him? How do you expect to be treated?

2. It is never too late to change because anyone can change if he desires to. What are some things you would like your significant other to change about his performance such as his approach on affection? Have you relayed your thoughts or opinions to him? If not, what are you afraid of?

3. If your significant other was being chivalric in the beginning of the relationship, but has stopped doing what he used to do for you, then why has he stopped? What are your plans to help him to start performing those same activities that were pleasing to you?

FIFTH KEY TO ACHIEVE PHYSICAL INTIMACY IS PROTECTION

One of the major roles a man has is to protect his woman. It is the man's responsibility to make the woman feel safe and secure. Women prefer men to be their protector. In layman terms, women NEED men to be our shield and make sure we are safe. Why? Women are vulnerable creatures. We are sensitive, caring, emotional, forgiving, strong, independent, beautiful, spiritual, and family-oriented human beings. Some women are independent and willing to do everything themselves. However, a God-fearing man takes the pressure off of us. We are putting it back in the man's hands which was God's intention in the first place when he created man and woman. *Genesis 2: 18* tell us, *"And the Lord God said, 'It is not good that man should be alone; I will make him a helper comparable to him.'"* God made the woman as a helpmate for man. Therefore, men are to protect, defend, care for and honor God's precious jewels—his women. If a man cannot make a woman feel safe and secure in the relationship, what good is he?

There is not one woman on the face of this planet who will say that she doesn't need a man to protect her. Protection is not only referring to prevention from bodily harm, but also protecting the family. The woman can feel threatened by other women or insecure in the relationship. *Protection* means not allowing another man or another person to disrespect your wife. *Protection* is defending your wife against any wrongful allegations or against any negativity that others might inflict on her. *Protection* is also making sure your wife does not engage in anything that will cause bodily harm, or put her in any dangerous situation. *Protection* is reassuring your wife how much you care about her, thus making her feel secure in the relationship. Finally, *protection* is covering your wife in prayer and interceding on her behalf. This is the most important function of a husband's role. You have to pray for her strength and faith because maintaining household and raising children are not easy. Keep her encouraged in prayer and encourage her in what you do and say to her.

Overall, women are seeking men who will meet all their needs: to feel secure, protected, covered in prayer and provided for. When a woman feels secure, the bond in your relationship will be stronger. In addition, the physical intimacy will be more enjoyable and special. A woman doesn't mind at all taking care of her man in the bedroom because he is taking care of her in areas where she needs it the most.

Ladies, I must say this: for the man to protect you, you have to let him. In other words, let the man do what he was born to do. The reason the man cannot do his job is that the woman will not let him. The woman is so busy complaining about what he isn't doing that she fails to look at what he is doing. Do not let this hinder your relationship. Open your eyes and see the good qualities he possesses--what a gift he is to you. Focus your attention on the things that he is doing and you will find that what he isn't doing is minuscule.

A man can only do what the woman allows him to do.

A man, who loves you and cherishes you, will take care of the household when you lose your job. God made man in His image and likeness. Therefore, the man has the ability to protect and care for you. All you have to do is submit to his authority.

The greatest example of protection is found in the book of Ruth. I like the book of Ruth and referenced from it in my debut book, *The Seven Deadly Sexual Sins*. The story of Ruth begins with an undemanding lady with a big heart. Ruth's mother-in-law, Naomi, loses everything and has to move to a new town to start over. Ruth lost her husband as well, who is Naomi's son, and she insists on going with Naomi and starting over with her. Ruth is faithful, obedient, and loyal to Naomi. Later, Ruth meets a wealthy man (through Naomi's doing) named Boaz, who acknowledges her self-worth, value, and vows to take care of her. *Ruth 2:9* reads, *"Let your eyes be on the field which they reap, and go after them. Have I not commanded the young men not to touch you? And when you are thirsty, go to the vessels and drink from what the young men have drawn."*

Boaz tells Ruth that he not only protected and shielded her from being harmed and scuffed by the men in the field, but she would also receive drinking water that the men have already drawn. Ruth did not have to work for anything. Whatever she needed, he provided. Boaz does not stop here. *Ruth 2:15-16* reads, *"And when she rose up to glean, Boaz commanded his young men, saying, 'Let her glean even among the sheaves, and do not reproach her. Also let grain from the bundles fall purposely for her; leave it that she may glean, and do not rebuke her.'"* This is an act of protection. Boaz even blesses her with more than she asked for. Ruth asked for the leftovers and Boaz blesses her with the overflow. He does not allow any of the men in the field to speak nastily about her or restrict her from her blessings. He is so protective of her that he will not allow anyone to get close to her without his permission. Overall, this is the type of man a woman needs—a man who will protect God's jewels from harm.

A godly man will give a woman more than what she needs or asks for. It's in his nature to do so.

Let's Stay Together with Protection

1. What are some things that make you feel secure and protected in your relationship? Is your significant other or spouse currently doing those things?

2. What are some things that make you feel insecure about your relationship? Are you insecure around other women, or is it his lack of attention or affection towards you, or is it the words he says to you that make you feel insecure?

3. What are you doing or saying to yourself that causes you to feel insecure or unprotected in your relationship? In other words, are you convincing yourself that he is having an affair? Are you convincing yourself that he doesn't love you? What causes you to feel unsure or unprotected?

SIXTH KEY TO ACHIEVE PHYSICAL INTIMACY IS PRODUCTION

Production is the next key to achieving real physical intimacy. Men who produce results and make things happen are qualities women look for in them. Someone *productive* means you are getting things done and moving in the right direction. *Productive* means you are not stagnant, but you are going somewhere and you are making progress. Women need men to take action and produce results. Women need men to go after things on their own, without any support from them. Men, think about these questions. What kind of drive and potential do you possess? How do you feel about where you are now? Do you want more out of life or are you content with where you are? We need to ask the men these questions in the beginning of a friendship.

If a man desires to make his woman happy but doesn't do anything to ensure his happiness such as starting his own business, then he is not living a fulfilled life. What about his happiness? What drives him out of bed every morning? What are the things that keep him dreaming and writing what he wants to do? These are some questions a man has to ask himself in order to fulfill his destiny. A man is not responsible for the woman's destiny and purpose. Each of us is in charge of his own destiny.

Each of us is in charge of his own destiny, so a man is not responsible for your destiny and you are not responsible for his.

It is great that a man wants to take care of his woman. He should provide for the household since it is his duty, but he cannot make the woman happy. If the woman operates in her life's purpose and the man operates in his, the couple will have a happy, fulfilled marriage. In order to produce anything, the man has to first plant the seed and then allows the seed to grow. Once the seed is planted and watered frequently, then a plant will begin to form.

God created man before he created woman. Once God created man, he gave man dominion and authority over the earth and then he created the woman. Man had authority before woman came into the picture. After the fall of man in the garden, God charges the man to work and provide for the woman. Subsequently, God gave Adam (man) dominion and power over everything and told him to provide. He would be able to provide for his wife and their future would be secure. Now, you see how important production is for the man. When a man cannot produce, it is like the seed that will not grow. No matter how many times he waters it, it still will not grow. Sometimes, he has to replant that seed again and again with a different fertilizer, which is the substance that makes it grow, until it finally grows. What I am saying is that a man will not produce unless he has it in himself to do so. If he has the faith, drive, potential, desire and the ability, he can produce; and whatever he produces, it will grow. An *unproductive man* yields undesirable results. He can become sterile and stagnant in the relationship, lacking the drive and passion to make the relationship grow and prosper.

Matthew 13:3 talks about the parable of the sower. This parable will shed light on the importance of being productive. *Matthew 13:3-8* reads, *"...Behold, a sower went out to sow. And as he sowed, some seed fell by the wayside; and the birds came and devoured them. Some fell on stony places, where they did not have much earth; and they immediately sprang up because they had depth of the earth. But when the sun was up they were scorched, and because they had no root they withered away. And some fell among thorns, and the thorns sprang up and choked them. But others fell on good ground and yielded a crop: some hundredfold, some sixty, some thirty."* The seeds are the Word of God, which fell on stony places by the wayside and on thorns that were eaten by the enemy. That seed was unproductive because a woman allowed negativity or an unproductive man to devour it, which was of no benefit or use to her. However, the seed (the Word) that fell on good ground grew and produced great results.

How your man speaks and what he says determines the success or failure of your relationship.

Be careful what type of man you ask for and what type of man you settle for because how he speaks determines what level of ground his seed will fall. If he speaks it, believes it, writes it, works to achieve it, then he can have it. If he doesn't believe it, he will never produce. A *faithless man* cannot produce because he does not believe he can. No one else will believe in him. A woman needs a man of faith and action because those two things will produce the desired results that she needs to have a healthy, prosperous marriage and a greater depth of intimacy. *"Faith without works is dead"* (*James 2:17*). It takes faith to begin, but works brings them into fruition. Remember that.

We just talked about the importance of the man sowing his seed on good ground by examining the

Parable of the Sower found in the book of Matthew. This particular parable dealt with the Word of God and how you received or processed the word would determine which ground level your seed fell on. Additionally, the man must also give abundantly to reap abundantly. *2 Corinthians 9:6* states, *"But this I say: He who sows sparingly will also reap sparingly, and he who sows bountifully will also reap bountifully."* There is also a similar scripture in Luke 6 that states that when we give, it will be given back to us in the same measure that we gave. So, giving is reciprocal. God says if you give to me, then I will in return, give it back to you. Therefore, these scriptures tell us in order to get great results and a high level of productivity, we must give abundantly. The more we give, the more it will be given back to us. There is no magic to the principle of giving other than we must give, which is hard for many of us because we don't know when or how we will get the return. If we had a definite date on when we could expect our return, then for many of us, giving would be so much easier. However, it takes faith out of the equation, which is a main requirement for our giving. We have to trust God in His Word that He will accomplish what He said. Sometimes, we yield unproductive results because of our level of giving. We don't like to give and when we do, we do it grudgingly and sparingly. When we do this, it is hard to reap any type of return because we gave with the wrong attitude. Once we get our attitude of giving right, then everything else will line-up.

If a person gives abundantly, he will reap abundantly. If a person gives sparingly, he will reap sparingly. Know your man's giving habits as that will determine his productivity level.

The Bible also says that God loves a cheerful giver and He honors our gift when we give it in the appropriate way. Along the same lines of giving, is being obedient to His Word by paying our tithe and offering as referenced in the book of Malachi. You will find a lot of biblical references related to giving because it is of the utmost importance to God. Giving shows Him what's in our hearts, mind, and spirit. It shows our character and how much faith and trust we have in God. It shows how much honor, respect and admiration we have for Him. The key to having a productive life is in our level of giving. If we raise the level of our giving, then God will raise the level in our productivity and we will produce so much that we will hardly be able to contain all that God will give to us.

So, to see the level of productivity in the man, look for how he speaks into your life and how he gives his money. If he speaks positively over you and gives abundantly to God by sowing and paying his tithe and offering, then he will produce great results. Examine your man's giving habits since this will determine his level of productivity. If he gives sparingly, then you will see that he is not seeing any results or receiving any returns because his giving does not line-up with the Word of God.

Now, ladies, we are talking about how important productivity is for a relationship because it lets you see what type of man you have in your life. *Productivity* is all about producing results and making things happen. A productive man should add to your life and not take anything away from it. Here are just a few tips to let you know if your significant other is a *freeloader* who subtracts from your life or a *producer* who adds to your life.

Tips that He's a Freeloader

1. He's a freeloader if he's always asking to borrow money from you and when you need something from him, he never has it. With him, it's "can I," "do you have," or "I need this," but he's never able to give back to you.

2. He's a freeloader if he's always complaining and whining about how bad things are for him and how things never go right for him. His talk is always negative and doom and gloom. He's constantly blaming other people for where he is and never takes responsibility for his own actions.

3. He's a freeloader if he's never able to pour anything back into your spirit, yet every time he needs solace, encouragement and comfort, you are right there. He never has a word of encouragement for you when you need it.

4. He's a freeloader if he acts jealous of your accomplishments or suddenly seems disinterested in any thing that you do. He is not your cheerleader or greatest supporter as he should be. Instead, he "rains on your parade" and makes you feel guilty about your accomplishments.

5. He's a freeloader if he doesn't know what his future goals or aspirations are and complacent about getting anything done. He has so many things he wants to do, but doesn't start any of them. He is constantly making excuses.

6. He's a freeloader if he is disorganized in his financial obligations and in his value of time. He is always late on his bills, always late going to work, always late picking you up for dinner

dates, or any type of planning activities, etc. He has no regard for time. He is just late for no reason at all. Or if he has a reason, it's a lame one.

7. He's a freeloader if he can't tell you where your relationship is headed. He can't tell you if he wants to marry you or if he just wants to date you. If you ever hear a man tell you that the two of you are just "kicking it" or just having fun, then those are signs he doesn't intend on marrying you. Also, if you ask him about marriage, you can never get a solid response from him. He's always saying he's not ready or it's not the right time or it will happen, but not right now. If he's constantly unsure about your future, then it means he is unsure about you and has no intentions on marrying you. Get out.

Tips that he's a Producer

1. He's a producer if he's constantly trying to find ways to earn money and to meet the basic needs of the household. He will work two jobs if necessary to provide for you and the household.

2. He's a producer if he speaks often of his goals and dreams and vision for the future and asks for your input and advice. He's constantly trying to make things happen and open his own doors. He is working consistently on his vision and purpose.

3. He's a producer if he doesn't wait for you to tell him what needs to be done. He takes the initiative to do things on his own. For example, if the dishes need washing, he will wash them without you asking him to do it.

4. He's a producer when he makes giving unto God his first priority. You don't have to question his obedience and faith to God because he leads the family in paying tithe and offering and makes it a priority in the relationship.
5. He's a producer if he leads his family in prayer and worship. He prays often for his family and covers his wife and children in prayer. He also leads his family in attending church regularly.
6. He's a producer when he speaks blessings and prosperity into the atmosphere. He tells his wife often how much he values and appreciates her and how special she is to him. He speaks that their marriage will prosper and that they will be blessed. He speaks positively over his household.
7. He's a producer when his friends and family members call on him a lot for advice and direction because they see he is headed somewhere. Other people who desire to lead will look to other leaders for counsel and support. Leaders lead others to lead.

If you see any of these freeloader signs in the relationship right now or a potential relationship in the person you will be dating, don't stick around for things to get better because they may not. I would suggest you exit the relationship because it will be draining and emotionally tiring on you. You will be stressed out trying to help someone who is unproductive because he is used to someone taking care of him and doesn't know how to take care of himself or anyone else. There are a lot of men who are freeloaders and they will drain you emotionally if you allow them to. Recognize these signs as potential roadblocks and address them immediately in the early stages of your relationship. A good man should always *add* to your life and bring something to the table, other than him. He should make your life better. If your life is more stressful with him in it, then get rid of him because he will drain the life out of you. Instead of *you* being better, you will become bitter and miserable. Avoid anyone who is not adding or depositing into your life. Look for the tips mentioned above to help you determine if he is a producer who will add to your life or if he is a freeloader who only subtracts from your life.

Let's Stay Together by Producing Results

1. Is your significant other a man of action who works hard to make things happen and gets the job done? Or is he complacent and stagnant and lacks drive and desire to work towards his goals?

2. What type of giver is your significant other? Does he give cheerfully and abundantly to God, or does he give grudgingly and sparingly? What things have you seen that lets you know what type of giver he is?

3. Examine the characteristics of your mate. Is he a *freeloader* who's always taking from you? Or is he a *producer* who adds and deposits into your life? What types of things does he do or say that makes you determine what type of man he is? What changes will you make going forward in your life if you discover that he does subtract from you and never deposits anything into you?

SEVENTH KEY TO ACHIEVE PHYSICAL INTIMACY IS PASSION

Yes, ladies love a man with intensity and passion. *Passion* is a desire, intensity, thirst, longing, and thrilling motivation that drives and pushes someone towards achieving whatever it is he cannot get out of his mind, no matter how hard he tries. It is there and will remain there until he does what he is passionate about. Without passion, it will be difficult for success to take place because he doesn't have what it takes inside of him to make it happen. The reason passion is so important in our relationship is because it comes from within. The intensity, strong liking, or desire for something all comes from inside of us. Therefore, a man needs to be passionate about his career, his relationship with his wife, and his relationship with God. Let's talk about all three of these qualities and how it will help improve the emotional and spiritual intimacy in your relationship.

A man needs to be passionate about his job. Men, if you don't like what you do, after working eight or more hours a day, you will have a hard time being passionate about anything else. A man's passion is what drives and motivates him, and pushes him to the next level. Don't confuse passion with obligation. A man's passion is not what gets him out of bed at 5:00 a.m. to go to work so he can provide for his family. He is not passionate about getting up early, but he does it out of obligation so he can provide for his family. If he doesn't mind getting out of bed at 5:00 a.m. to do what he enjoys doing, this shows that he is passionate about what it is he is getting up for.

> Passion stems from doing something you **desire** to do. Obligation stems from doing something you **have** to do.

If passion comes from a desire and you do not like your job, then one can presume that you have no passion about your job. This does not mean you are not a passionate person; it only means that you have no passion or drive for your job. You need to get out of it and do something that you are passionate about, or you will be miserable and resentful. I feel this way about my current job. I dread going to work. I feel unmotivated and uninspired to work. I cannot wait for the day to be over because there is no intensity or drive inside of me. The only thing that gets me up at 6:00 a.m. is the fact that I have to go to work because I have financial obligations I have to meet.

What I dream about every night, think about everyday, even at work, and what I write in the late night hours are the things I am passionate about. These are the things that drive me to get up because I have other things to look forward to and to strive towards. Moreover, I know soon that my change will come. I will fulfill my purpose by writing books, starting my own Christian magazine, hosting my own television show, hosting my own radio talk show, starting a business, building a homeless shelter, and speaking at seminars and workshops. These are some things that I am passionate about.

When a person is passionate about something, he/she will do whatever it takes to make it happen. He/She may miss a few hours of sleep, or sacrifice more time and energy to see it come to pass. In addition, a person can create a financial burden to meet the sacrifices to fulfill his purpose or destiny. This is Satan's tactic to place fear in your path once you discover your calling and purpose in life. Why? Because a man or woman with purpose is a person with a desire to fulfill God's calling. Moreover, a man or woman will not ignore the desires inside of him/her and will begin to take an active role to see the purpose come to fruition. Whether it takes five or fifteen years to fulfill your destiny, you will do it because of the desire placed inside of you.

> You will lose your passion if you don't use it. Use it or lose it.

A man needs to have passion towards his wife. Does he still have intimate feelings for his wife after ten years of marriage? Does he tell her often how attractive she is and how he cannot wait to get home after work because he knows she is waiting for his return? Remember passion is that intensity, fire, and deep longing for something or someone that all comes from within. If a man has passion for his lady, she will see the passion in his eyes and observe his actions in the bedroom. Why? The bedroom is where you can release all of your attraction, longing, desire, and passionate intensity towards someone else. When this happens, the lovemaking session you have will be great. It won't be sex as usual. Women have an intuitive feeling and will definitely know if her mate is sincere.

Another way she can tell if her husband has passion is how he kisses her. Are the kisses soft and sensual and filled with desire? Most times, the kisses that the woman receives are goodbye and greeting kisses, which are the little pecks on the lips when she leaves and returns home from work. Every now and then, the man has to give a real, "I want you kiss" to let her know that she is still desirable and still turns him on.

A kiss also expresses affection towards your mate. If your mate does not kiss you anymore or he does not want to hold your hand in public, then where is the affection? If he only displays affection in the bedroom, is this fulfilling or do you beg for more? For some women, this is enough affection, but for others, they need more. Let me expound on the importance of kissing since there are many of you who do not even kiss your spouse anymore. You come home from a long day's work and go straight to the sofa, or take off your clothes while in the bedroom without even greeting your spouse with a kiss. What happened to the passionate kiss to express how valuable and loveable you are to your spouse?

I mentioned the importance of kissing briefly in my first book, but let's take a look at the biblical significance and why it is important in achieving physical, emotional, and spiritual intimacy in our relationship. In *Luke 7*, it explains about a woman who kisses the feet of Jesus and anoints them with scented oil. This is a sign of worship, respect, and praise to him because she recognized who he was. The Pharisees were so upset that Jesus was letting this "sinful" woman touch him because of who she was. When Jesus realized what they were thinking, he was upset. *Luke 7: 44-45* reads, *"Do you see this woman? I entered your house; you gave Me no water for My feet, but she has washed My feet with her tears and wiped them with the hair of her head. You gave Me no kiss, but this woman has not ceased to kiss My feet since the time I came in."*

This Scripture elaborates on kissing. I want to highlight what Jesus is saying about kissing. In *Luke 7*, the word *kiss* is mentioned three times. First, *kissing* represents respect and authority. Second, *kissing* represents acknowledgment and greetings. Lastly, *kissing* is a sign of affection and attention. Jesus responded to Simon, who was a Pharisee and whose home Jesus was invited to, that he did not do what was customarily done when you invite someone to your home. You have to kiss a person who enters your home of which is a sign of respect, acknowledgment, and affection. Simon, the Pharisee, did not do this. He failed to show Jesus any attention, respect, and consideration. However, when a "sinful" woman did, Jesus' heart was open to receiving and forgiving this woman of her sins.

Ladies and gentlemen, kissing on a regular basis is what you must do in your relationships. Do you respect and love your spouse? If you do, you will show it by kissing him/her and letting him/her know how much passion and desire you have for him/her.

One final scripture on kissing is *1 Peter 5: 14* reads, *"Greet one another with a kiss of love."* Do you see this? This scripture says to *greet*, meaning acknowledge or recognize that person. Not only does it say to acknowledge or show respect, but it also says do it with a kiss of love. Wow! So, you mean to tell me that kissing is a biblical principle and isn't something we came up with? All this time I was not showing my spouse respect, love, and acknowledgement by not kissing him and it was God's will for me to do so. Once you know better, you will do better.

Moving forward, it is okay to kiss him often, but keep in mind that you must do it in respect, love, and because you care about the person you're kissing. In other words, kiss only your spouse. Even if you are in a dating relationship, only kiss him because he is going to become your future husband. Otherwise, you will end up kissing a whole lot of frogs. I want to point out that frogs are nasty, ugly, and undesirable creatures. You know the saying about kissing frogs. Therefore, I used this metaphor so you can think about how many times you were "grossing" yourself out by kissing all those "frogs". My co-workers hate when I say this word, but I'm going to say it. "That's nasty!" Lol.

> By giving kisses to anyone so easily is like losing your respect. Cherish each kiss as you love and respect yourself.

To sum it up, women (wives) like affection and attention and any lack of it indicates to us that you are not interested and do not love us anymore. Remember, women need to feel secure in the relationship. Our mates need to do certain things to make us feel secure. When we do not feel secure in the relationship, we can sense that something is wrong and suspect you are cheating. When a man is unfaithful to us, we try to ignore it or tell ourselves that we are imagining things. Moreover, we sense something is wrong.

There are some things a man can do to help his woman to feel secure. He can also demonstrate his passion regularly on those dating nights. This indicates a man's passion and desire to spend time with us, which showcases that we are important and valuable in his life. He can take his wife on a date to enjoy all the things she loves to do: laugh and have a good time enjoying each other's company.

Passion also stems from excitement. Have fun with your spouse or potential spouse. Don't be too serious and uptight that you don't allow yourself to enjoy each other's company and have a good time. Forget about those little things that get on your nerves, the nagging and fussing, and just have fun together. Do silly activities together such as water balloon fighting or water gun fighting, pillow fighting, get on the swings at the park, or race to see who can climb the monkey bars faster and so forth. I know you still have that kid in you, so let it come out and just have fun.

Couples concentrate so much on the financial strains, disagreements, and differences of opinion that they fail to take time to simply have fun and enjoy each other. Again, passion shouldn't always come from your bedroom, but it should also show in your creativity and adventurous habits. Doing fun things together shows the person not only do you love him/her, but also you like him/her. Doing silly things like the ones I mentioned above show your significant other that you like him. In other words, you enjoy being around that person. You enjoy being goofy or silly, and just letting loose and having a great time. You will find out that your mate is silly as well and he/she loves to laugh and have fun too. Put the fun and excitement back in your marriage or relationship and enjoy one another. Everything doesn't have to be so serious all the time. You have a sense of humor, so use it and you will see a profound difference in your relationship. You will draw closer to each other once you realize how much you enjoy each other's company.

Remember to enjoy each other and have fun. Chill out, relax, and just let go. Bring the fun back in your relationship.

I heard many married women complain that their husbands don't spend time with them anymore. Their husbands do not send flowers, take them on vacations, or some of the things he did to woo her. Then, she tells her girlfriends how she noticed that he has changed after they got married. She also assumed he would continue romancing her, but he stopped after a few years of their marriage. Why is that husbands? Why does the romance end when you get married? In my opinion, the romance begins when you get married. However, after speaking to a few married women, they will tell you that things have changed and it's not what it used to be.

You have to keep the romance alive, whether it is two years of marriage or twenty years. We still like flowers, cards, dates, perfume, and those things that wooed us. We have not changed. We still desire those same things you did for us when we were dating. We want you to continue splurging and doing those small basic things to keep us feeling secure in the relationship. This reminds us that you still desire us.

Some will argue that people do change and grow apart, especially if your marriage is rocky or shaky. If you and your spouse are having problems in the marriage, I would presume that the romance will vary because you are growing apart. Communication can be an issue. You are not conversing with your partner like you used to. When people change in a negative way, it explains the absence of flowers, candy, gifts, etc., because your husband does not value those things to woo you or make you feel special in the relationship anymore.

> Some people change for the better and some for the worse. Recognize what type of change is taking place in your relationship.

If this is you right now and you know that things have changed, I would advise you go back to the root of the problem. What were some of the things that you shared when you first loved your significant other? Think about all of those things that made you fall in love with him and then see if those things are still present. If there are mutual feelings, you have a strong chance in making the marriage work. If not, you will have to work harder or possibly move on. Sometimes, we get into relationships that just don't work no matter what we do. Sometimes, we are involved in relationships to avoid being alone or out of obligation or convenience. If this is the case and there are no chances of reconciliation, then separation or divorce may be your answer. Seek God first before you do anything!

Let's look at passion relating to rejection. How can passion stem from a person's rejection? A woman who says "no" to a man's request to date isn't always the final result. If a man really wants her, then he should go after her. What type of passion or drive does he possess if he walks away? Passion is a drive, intensity, and desire that come from within. If a person has passion, it will also show outwardly. In order words, how bad do you want it? If the woman is worth the pursuit and the chase, then it's the man's responsibility to win her affection. For example, when a man truly likes a woman and feels that there's something special and unique about her, he will ask her out on a date. But if she says no, the man should not allow this response of a "no" to deter him from pursuing her.

> Ladies, if a man is trying to pursue you, let him and see where it leads.

There are so many things that a man can do to pursue a woman to let her know that he is sincere about spending time with her. Here are a few examples: a man can talk to her dear friend or an acquaintance to find out where she works and send her flowers or candy or "coincidentally" meet her at the gym, workplace, or grocery store where she normally goes. By doing these simple things, you will get a woman's attention because she likes the pursuit and the chase. It makes her feel special, desirable, and valuable. Women love affection and attention from the opposite sex. To go even further, I would say that women NEED affection and attention because it is part of our genetic makeup. Without it, we will feel disconnected, unloved, unwanted, unappreciated, and under-valued and the absence of these lead to many other internal issues such as low self-esteem, depression, and loneliness. We enjoy being chased, desired and wanted. It makes us feel special and affirms our value. It also increases our confidence level when we know we "got it going on!"

Here's a real life story: Eight years prior, I worked with a young lady who caught the attention of a young man at the workplace. We were bank tellers. The young man desired to spend time with her and asked her out on a date. She declined because she didn't want to enter into another relationship after recently breaking up from her boyfriend. A few days later, the young man sent her a bouquet of beautiful flowers. Later, I noticed that the young lady started putting on lipstick and makeup, whenever she knew he was coming to the bank. I believed the flowers impressed her because she thought he gave up after she rejected him, but he sent flowers to signify that he wasn't going away unless she was not interested in him and pushed him away. But, if he had a slight chance to be a part of her life, he pursued her with passion and his purpose was to get to know her. I never knew if they dated; however, I did notice subtle changes in her appearance and personality that resulted from the flowers he sent her.

Sometimes, a woman says no to a man's request to date or call to see how interested he really is. Maybe she desires to be chased and pursued and for the man to try harder to get her attention: to see his passion for her and how much he likes her. If he's persistent and diligent and does whatever it takes to let the woman know that he is really interested in her, then she will likely say yes to him because his request is genuine and sincere. A man won't work hard for something that he doesn't really want. If it requires too much work for him, then he will likely give up and leave.

A man won't pursue a woman that he really doesn't want because pursuing takes time and effort, and he will walk away if he's not really interested.

Today, men are making minimal efforts in chasing and pursuing women because women are pursuing the men and asking them out on a date. This is shown on the dating reality shows on television and dating sites on the Internet. Women are vying for the affection from men when men should be chasing after women. What ever happened to the thrill of being chased and pursued and to feel desired and special? What ever happened with the man sending a woman flowers, letters, cards, or candy until she accepted his dinner request? What ever happened to a woman waiting on her mate instead of taking charge of her own life and destiny? What happened is that a woman began settling for any man by lowering her standards where she threw her morals and values out the window. Once a woman did that, then it made it much easier for a man to get into her heart and in her bed because she was unaware of her value and self-worth. Therefore, anyone who showed her some attention, she fell for the lies as if it was authentic. She didn't care if it was the wrong type of attention such as admiring her physical appearance, just as long as she was getting noticed. She settled for less by letting her guards down until she lowered her standards to his level.

We are marrying someone beneath our means and abilities. This is why there are so many relationships dissolving and marriages are falling apart at an alarming rate. We settled to meet our physical needs, but not our emotional and spiritual needs. Therefore, there is a chemical imbalance in the relationship, where the couple is *unequally yoked*, meaning one person is a believer (righteous person) and the other is not. Both of you have to be equal in your beliefs and in your Christian faith. Couples who are unequally yoked start to share feelings of unhappiness and discontentment. They begin to feel disconnected from one another and there is no longer unity in the relationship. Without passion, the relationship will never survive because if he doesn't want to make the relationship work, it won't work. A *passionless man* is not someone you want to associate with because his lack of drive, passion, or intensity will never produce anything worthwhile. If he doesn't desire it, he won't work for it.

Being *equally yoked* means the both of you are equal in your beliefs and in your Christian faith.

Finally, a man has to be passionate about God. There are three areas that will determine his passion for God. Please review each area to see where his passion lies and determine where he needs improvement.

The first area to determine his passion towards God is by reviewing his living standards. Is he living to serve God or man? When you *serve God*, it means you take on a Christian approach. When you *serve man*, you take on the things of the world and do things that are worldly and against God's will. *Being a Christian* means you are Christ-like and you possess the same characteristics as Jesus Christ. We know according to the Bible, our characteristics are exemplifying the life example of Jesus, who encompassed caring, honesty, giving, forgiveness, and loving others. In addition, we know that Jesus showed great compassion to others whether they deserved it or not. These characteristics should also be displayed as a follower of Jesus Christ. When you embody these traits, it demonstrates how passionate you are about God. You are surrendering your ways to be like God; to be what He desires us to be as the Bible explains it. If we love God with our body, heart, mind, and soul, this will clearly show that we are living examples of Christ and will continue to do what it takes to please God instead of ourselves. Moreover, we become mindful of our choices and decisions, and make a conscientious effort to obey God's Word. Our actions should speak louder than our words.

> *Being passionate for God* means we love Him with our whole body, heart, mind, and soul.

John 12:26 reads, *"If anyone serves me, let him follow Me; and where I am, there My servant will be also. If anyone serves Me, him My father will honor."* To *serve* means to respect, honor, and obey. It also means *walking in obedience* to what God has called us to do and an act of giving of oneself to the care and concern of another person. By serving God with honor, obedience and faith show we can identify ourselves as a follower of Him.

Secondly, your giving shows your passion for God. The Bible tells us that God loves a cheerful giver. Those who don't like to give show that they are not followers of Jesus Christ. Jesus' whole life was an act of giving and serving others. Jesus healed, delivered, ministered, gave, sacrificed, suffered, comforted, forgave, and much more because He loved us. He demonstrated His love for all of us through His giving; therefore, the same is required of those who are followers of Christ.

The Bible also says that tithing and offering are not the only gifts to honor God, but also our time and talents. We can give our time to those who are in need of our service and work in the area of our gift or talent that God has bestowed upon us. Whether it's teaching Sunday school, volunteering in our community, working at a daycare, ministering, or whatever gift or talent we possess, we must use it for the glory of God. Although we donate to charities or tithe to the church we attend, it is also vital for us to use our time wisely to allow our resources and spiritual gifts to serve many. Remember, there is someone in the world that needs our gifts and talents, and if we don't use them, we will miss the opportunity to help someone else to complete what God purposed for them to do.

Lastly, our passion towards God is demonstrated in how we communicate to others about God and how we talk to God about how we feel about Him. Are we sharing the good news about God to others? Are we praising and worshipping God and constantly giving thanks to Him for what He has done, already doing and what He will do? Do we believe in God's Word by speaking words of affirmation and confirmation to others? If we are doing these things on a consistent basis, we are demonstrating our passion for God. As believers, we are mandated by God to speak about Him to others so that we can lead those who are lost to Christ. It's difficult to remain silent when God has blessed us and has done marvelous things in our lives. Some people call it "testifying." *Testifying* is sharing verbally the goodness of the Lord and what He's done for us and how far God has brought us. It is also a testament of our faith and commitment to God by letting others know that He is real. Our testimony will allow others to believe in God, and be converted and transformed into a new creature in Christ.

Your *testimony* comes from passing your tests and sharing with others how you did it.

If you are willing to serve in any capacity at your local church or in your community, your personal relationship with God will become stronger and you will develop a closer relationship with Him. When you talk about God regularly to others, have discussions about the Word of God, and give your testimony to others, these demonstrate your passion for God. If you serve with your time, tithe, and/or talent, you will help to advance God's kingdom.

Please re-examine where your relationship with God is and which area requires sharpening to improve your relationship with God. Do you need improvement in how you live, how you communicate about God to others, or how you give? How do you work on improving your passionate level towards God? You can improve your relationship with God by praying, reading your Bible daily, fasting or consecrating yourself, and attending church regularly. As you do these things, you will mature in your walk with Christ. Gradually, you will notice a change took place within you and your desires will begin to shift. As you mature as a believer in Christ, you can invite your mate to grow with Him too.

As a couple, you should share these intimate, spiritual moments in the presence of God together and your relationship with each other will grow stronger. *Ecclesiastes 4: 9, 12* reads, *"Two are better than one, because they have a good reward for their labor."* Verse 12 reads, *"Though one may be overpowered by another, two can withstand him. And a threefold cord is not quickly broken."* A three strand cord cannot be easily broken when you attach God as the third strand. God is the glue that holds things together and without the glue, a marriage will not withstand all the ups and downs that a couple will face. It is extremely difficult for one person to fight alone. Both of you have to be willing to fight for your marriage together. If one of you feel faint or tired, then that's when you will have to include the third strand, who is God, to help you through those tough times and situations.

It is also vital that the both of you continue seeking God together through praying and fasting even when times are good. This serves as a constant reminder that God's grace and mercy will sustain the relationship. Some marriages fall apart so quickly because we call on God too late or when the problems or situations are beyond repair. Well, let me just add that with God all things are possible and He can repair anything. What I meant by saying it is too late or beyond repair is that when you become emotionally unattached from the relationship, then your mind is already set on divorce and getting out of it. I advise couples to pray constantly for each other, with each other, and pray individually to strengthen their marriage. So when the storms arise, you are better equipped to handle them. By consistently praying and seeking God for the solution, God will heal the marriage.

As a couple, you will mature together by including God in the relationship regardless of what level of growth he is in. If you grow and he remains unchanged, you will have problems connecting spiritually with each other.

Moreover, our emotional and spiritual intimacy stems from the passion and desire that each feels, and when these two things are present, it will form a tighter bond that will not be easily broken. This is what *chemistry* is all about. *Chemistry* is connecting with each other spiritually, emotionally, and physically. If either of these areas is off balance, then you will see conflicts in the relationship. The passion and desire you have for one another will connect the two of you closer because of the sincere feelings that you have for each other. This will not only display in the bedroom, but also in your relationship with God and at your job.

Let's Stay Together with Passion

1. Does your spouse express his passion and desire for you on a regular basis? How does he/she display it? What are some of the things he/she does to show his passions and desires for you?

2. Do you believe that a person can show too much passion or desire for someone else? If so, why is it too much? In other words, this person is overly kissing, hand holding, hugging, and laying on you? Explain when it is overly or not enough passion and desire shown.

3. What are some things that you have learned about passion that you didn't know before? How will you use these basic revelations about passion in your relationship today to enhance the level of intimacy with your spouse?

EIGHTH KEY TO ACHIEVE PHYSICAL INTIMACY IS PARTICIPATION

The eighth key to achieve physical intimacy is participation. A woman desires a man who actively participates in their discussions and offers his opinions or advice. The man engages in conversation and is interested in what his woman has to say. However, if he acts as if he cannot wait for her to stop talking as if she's boring him to death, then this can be a problem for the woman since she is an emotional and expressive human being. A woman likes to talk, but she needs a man who enjoys hearing her and listening to what she is saying. Listening demonstrates that he cares by paying attention to her. She feels better.

I agree with the chapter in Steve Harvey's book, *Act like a Lady and Think like a Man*, where he states that men don't like to talk and they clam up when their women suggest they need to talk. This is true that men avoid serious conversations with their women, especially if the women suggest that they need to talk, but men, in general, love to talk. When a woman suggests that she needs to talk to her man, it is only because he isn't paying attention to the previous conversations that they've already had. Usually, when the woman suggests they need to talk, it is something that they have already discussed, but haven't worked out yet. Maybe the conversation got interrupted or maybe they didn't come to a final agreement, but the woman suggests to the man they need to talk because she is still thinking about what is bothering her that they haven't completely dealt with yet. She wants to seek out resolutions, whereas he wants to ignore it, forget about it, and move on.

It's not so simple for the woman because she is emotionally attached to the situation. She needs closure and reassurance more than the man does. It is usually not something new that they are discussing, but rather a past situation. In the woman's mind, she has to resolve it or she will have a difficult time moving on. When a woman suggests to her man they need to talk, more often than not, he knows what they need to talk about. He was secretly hoping that his woman forgot about the issue so they wouldn't have to deal with it. That's why men clam up when we suggest the conversation because men tend to sweep things under the rug and view it as "no big deal," but for women, it is a big deal, especially if he ignores us and acts nonchalant about it. We process things differently than men. It's in our genetic makeup that we are sensitive, caring, emotional, and nurturing human beings. So, we care about things that a lot of men don't care about or view as unimportant, but to us, it is. Ladies, am I right? Go on ladies and high-five another sister if you are sitting next to one or shout, "you've got that right!"

Men have to learn and understand women's emotional habits. Be a little more sensitive to their needs and concerns and address those concerns instead of trying to selfishly ignore them hoping that she forgets about what's bothering her. For example, something simple as the man putting the toilet seat down before he leaves the bathroom is what the woman wants to discuss. He knows it too because she has mentioned it to him over and over again. Since he is not listening or being sensitive to her needs, she finally suggests that they need to talk about this issue and fix the problem. The man was hoping that his woman would deal with the toilet seat issue and just continue to put it down for him and not say anything. But if something is bothering a woman, she will eventually say something to him. It may take her a few weeks or even months until she gets irritated and frustrated and asks him to talk because she wants the problem fixed, not ignored as he has done previously.

So, when a woman tells her man they need to talk, it doesn't have to be something serious or deep, but things that are bothering her that she wants to get off her chest. It may not even have to do with him, but a situation she is dealing with and she just needs a listening and caring man to console and comfort her. Men, how hard is that? Just being there and available is what most women want from you.

A dear friend and I talked about these things and this was one main issue she was having in her relationship. The lack of communication with her spouse was irritating her, draining her and getting her so annoyed and upset that she didn't know what to do. She was tired of arguing and tired of discussing the same issue over and over again, so finally, she just let it go and let God. Sometimes, that's really all you need to do is stop trying to fix it yourself and let God do it for you. Amen! Again, communication is so important in a relationship. You have to learn how to express your feelings to each other and then come to some type of common ground or agreement. When only one person is doing all the talking and the other is not listening, then that's a problem. I'm not talking about just hearing what is being said, but actually understanding what is being said. That is a big difference. I hope she doesn't mind me learning from her and sharing this with you as I believe the lack of communication is a huge problem in many marriages. I listened to her and I totally understood what she was saying even though I have never been in a relationship. Communication is major factor in the success and failure of your marriage. Thank you sista girl for sharing this with me. I know you are not the only one frustrated with the lack of communication in your relationship. Some people have a dysfunction when it comes to communicating and expressing themselves and they just don't know how to communicate at all. I have no answer for that type of person. I will tell you that it's going to be a difficult relationship, but all things are possible with God. I'm praying for you, my dear friend, and all those who are married and are reading this book that God will work on healing the broken communication in your marriage and I hope that this book will be their starting point for healing to take place.

> When a woman suggests "let's talk" to her man, she only wants his undivided attention that he has failed to give her previously.

Men prefer to talk about things that interest them. For example, there are more men who are weather forecasters than women. Men also dominate in the career as sports newscasters than women. In addition, there are more men working in sales than women. Therefore, men enjoy talking, but the problem is they would like to discuss subjects or topics that interest them. Men: how would you feel if you wanted to talk to your woman about your day, a sports event, or workout session and she ignored you? You would be upset because you would want her to participate in a conversation of which you are passionate about, but instead, you get the cold shoulder. Well, that's what we need you to do for us. Participation is about conversing and listening. We can have effective communication without any problems such as arguing and fighting.

There are some of you who can not communicate with your spouse because everything you say or don't say becomes an argument. It could be that you just don't see eye-to-eye anymore. Moreover, both of you have grown apart and no longer respect each other the way you used too. It could also be his lack of participation. You are doing all the talking and he has not offered any feedback. He is not attentive and you become highly upset. Men, we need a partner that is open to discussions and shares things with us. If there is no sharing, we do not have a partnership. What we have is a sole proprietorship. If we are going to feel like we are in the relationship by ourselves, then we may as well be by ourselves. What's the point in having a relationship if there is no participation?

We need to talk to you daily, even if for a brief moment, because like I said, women are sensitive and emotional creatures. We need to feel wanted, loved, and needed. Moreover, we are asking you to participate in the conversation. Besides, we know what you are thinking and we can see where your mind is at. Talk to us. Tell us how your day went, what you want for dinner, what your plans are for the week, or whatever else is on your mind because we don't mind listening. Participating in the conversation also allows you to get your needs met. We cannot meet your needs if we don't know what your needs are. *Matthew 7: 7* tells us, *"ask, and it will be given to you."* To get anything from God, we first must ask Him. If we don't ask, we will not receive.

We cannot meet our man's needs if he doesn't tell us what his needs are.

If you ask for something, you must expect to receive something, right? For example, when I ask my friend to lend me twenty dollars, I am asking in hopes of receiving this money. Therefore, asking is so important in our relationship with God because by asking, the doors are open to receiving. The same concept applies in our relationships. We need to have open and honest communication with our spouse so we have a greater depth of understanding about each other and also improve the emotional and spiritual intimacy in the relationship.

Finally, the importance of participation is that our words are powerful. What is spoken over the family is what will be. So, you have to be careful what you speak into the atmosphere because our words are powerful. In *Genesis 1* when God spoke "let there be," it was so. Moreover, we long for a man to speak blessings, prosperity, wealth, and good health over the woman. The Bible says we have to speak those things that are not as though they are. In other words, speak positively over a negative situation. This role is so important in the household because if the man is the head of the house, his words should demonstrate his authority and position in the woman's life.

Proverbs 15:23 reads, *"A man has joy by the answer of his mouth, and a word spoken in due season, how good it is!"* Even when things are going bad at your job, the children are misbehaving and the marriage is falling apart, someone needs to speak "life" to your gloomy situation. Someone needs to believe that things will get better. Not necessarily does the man have to do everything; however, the wife should have enough faith and power to speak blessings and peace over the household too. All it takes is for someone to believe in what he/she is speaking. A word spoken at the right time will lift your spirits and give you the faith you need to move forward and strengthen you to press on.

> Your husband should be able to speak life to you and comfort you when you need comforting.

Having a man of faith is very important in your relationship because when things are not going so well, you are going to need someone who has the power, authority, and faith to edify the relationship and speak positively. Everything will work out because if you can speak and believe it, you can have what was spoken. Another Scripture that speaks on the importance of our words is *Proverbs 25:11* and it reads, *"A word fitly spoken is like apples of gold in settings of silver."* Wow! First, a word spoken must come from God. It cannot be any word that you pulled out of the air randomly. It has to be given to you by God, for the word to work in the person's life that you are speaking over. Lastly, the reference to *gold* refers to divinity and *silver* refers to redemption. Not only will the word that God gave you bring everlasting life, it will also redeem or save you from sin. The *Word of God* is redeeming, cleansing, and everlasting. The importance of participation draws us toward intimacy because we have to listen more, converse effectively by actively engaging in the conversation and speak positively into each other's lives. If you can do those things, then the emotional and spiritual connection will surely be stronger because you both are on the same page and have strengthened the bond between the two of you—what was spoken and believed for in your heart.

Let's Stay Together with Participation

1. What are some major communication problems that you and your spouse are dealing with currently? How will you begin applying what you have learned about effective communication to resolve those issues?

2. Which one is the talkative, expressive person in the relationship? What does this person talk about most of the time? What is this person's mood: are they soft-spoken, upbeat, uplifting, or encouraging, or show signs of anger, resentment, frustration, and so forth? If the communication is more negative than positive, then what are some things you can do to change your language?

3. Where do you and your spouse communicate most frequently? Do you believe that your area of communication has a positive or negative impact on the intimacy in your relationship? In answering this question, think about the areas where you dominated the conversation such as the kitchen, bedroom, living room, dining room, and does the location have a direct impact on what type of communication you have. For example, if you communicate most in the living room, is the television on?

NINTH KEY TO ACHIEVE PHYSICAL INTIMACY IS PROVIDING

The ninth key to achieving real physical intimacy is having a man who can provide. A woman needs a family provider. When the family's needs are met, his needs will be met. It's reciprocal. If he takes care of you, then you should take care of him. Providing does not only refer to financial needs as there are countless ways that he can provide for his woman aside from finances. Even though most women prefer men to be financially secured or either headed in that direction, there are many women who are the breadwinners or financial providers as men take care of the children. They are attending to the children while their wives work. They are still providers because they are meeting a need. Other ways men can provide for their wives are cooking, cleaning, shopping for groceries, doing the laundry, helping the children with their homework, or transporting them to and from school. These are ways a man can provide for the household besides contributing financially. Money is not that important to women as men think. I didn't say it wasn't important, but not that important. We don't want a broke man. A woman is content with a man who loves God, loves his family, helps out in the community, and makes a decent, honest living. We do not want someone who is cheap, arrogant, or does not attend church. I would be much happier with a man who has a heart for God than a rich man who is self-centered, evil, and cheap. *Proverbs 28:6* reads, *"Better is the poor who walks in his integrity than one perverse in his ways, though he be rich."*

There are some women who will settle for men with money because they feel it will make them happy. Some women would rather accept mess rather than struggle financially. They tolerate his bickering, verbal abuse, infidelities, lying, and inconsiderate ways as long as they can shop at Saks, buy a Louis Vuitton purse, get their monthly spa massages and pedicures, eat at the finest restaurants and drive a Mercedes Benz. For those women who settle for money, they are trying to compensate for what is missing on the inside of them. Internally, they are struggling, but they try to cover up the emptiness they feel on the inside by buying what is available to them on the outside. What I am trying to point out is that financial stability is important in the relationship, but it is not what the relationship should be built on. You'll go spiritually and emotionally bankrupt if you build your relationship on money. When the money runs out, prayer will sustain you. Think about it.

As stated earlier, there are many different ways a man can provide besides financially. In other words, if the husband suddenly gets laid off at his job, and now his wife is the sole financial provider, then the husband still has the responsibility to provide for his wife. He should not be lying on the couch watching television when she gets home from work. He should have the house cleaned, dinner prepared, kids picked up from school, etc. He should also be looking for a job or some way to make some income even if it's not as much income as he would like. A real man will find a way to provide for his family. All the real men who are reading this book do this: throw your hands in the air and wave 'em like you just don't care. Ha, Ha.

> A man who is a *provider* meets the needs of the household. Providers find ways to provide for the home.

Ladies, we cannot always look at the financial aspect of the man. Yes, he needs to have a steady job and income, but if something happens in which he no longer has it, then he should still find ways to provide for his family and make sure the family's needs are met.

It's comical and hilarious when you meet a man that the first thing he asks a woman is "What are you bringing to the table?" I had a young man ask me what I was offering him and what was I bringing to the table. However, I find it odd that in today's society where a man wants a woman to be the provider when God strictly requires him to be in charge. In the Book of Genesis, God told Adam to work and till the ground to provide for his family and he told the woman to be fruitful and multiply. How does a man have the audacity to ask a woman what she is bringing to him when the responsibility of providing, protection, planning, and all the other principles that are listed in this book rest on the man? What kind of man will ask a woman to take care of him? Not any man that I want.

Ladies, let's talk about this a bit more. Before a man pursues you, he should have a table laid out for you. He needs to have several dishes on his table that you can eat from: job, house, car, good credit, savings account, business venture, ministry leader, loves God, community organizer, gives to charity, takes good care of his children if he has some, maintains his health, knows how to treat you and is very chivalrous, values you and respects you, etc. These are some things to look for in a man that's pursuing a wife. He may not have everything she wants him to have on the table, but he should have some of the things she needs and what he doesn't have, his woman should be able to fill in the missing dishes. A woman complements a man by adding to what he already has. The key is this: a man has a table prepared with dishes ready to serve her, and if not, then she needs to know that she's sitting at the wrong table. Ladies, if there is nothing on his table, get up and leave. A man cannot pursue you if he has nothing to offer you. Remember ladies: he should be bringing something to you other than himself.

> A man should pursue a woman and show her what "dishes" he has prepared for her on his table.

A man who is strong, God-fearing, intelligent, and caring is what a woman looks for in a man. A provider will provide for his queen. He doesn't want her stressing out about the bills, but he will be there for her so she knows they're in this together. A woman was created to be the man's helper, not his provider. She helps him, aids him, guides him, prays for him, strengthens him, and encourages him so he can be the man God intended for him to be. *"And the Lord God said, "It is not good that man should be alone; I will make him a helper comparable to him" (Genesis 2:18).* Most of you are familiar with this scripture, but I believe you fail to realize what it truly means. Before woman ever came into the picture, there was man. Man was made first. Man was large and in charge until one day, God saw something that was missing in Adam's life and He created woman. The woman was created to help the man. When you help someone else, you're helping him to do what he already should be doing. In other words, you are helping him do something because two people can get something done quicker and easier than one person can.

> **Woman was created to be a helper to her man.**

God didn't say that Adam was incapable of doing it solo. He had the capabilities, but he needed the assistance and that is where woman came into existence. Overall, a woman is to help her man to perform his job, not to do his job for him. This is where a woman messes up. Instead, she started taking the lead and doing the man's job. This is not what God intended. She is out of her natural scope and league. God created man to lead and the woman is to help him lead the way. How is she helping the man? She is helping her man to do his job by supporting him, praying for him, and making sure his physical, emotional, and spiritual needs are met. Basically, she is to be there for him. Whatever the man needs to be "the man," she is there to help him do his job.

Let's Stay Together with a Provider

1. Aside from providing for you and your family financially, what are other ways that your significant other or spouse provides for you?

2. Think about the role you are playing in your spouse's life. Are you the helper as God created you to be or are you operating as the leader? If you are operating as the leader of the household, what are some things you are doing in the leadership role and why isn't the man participating in his lead role?

3. What are some specific traits or characteristics that you look for in a man to verify if he is a provider or not? In other words, what are some things he brought to the table upon meeting you?

TENTH KEY TO ACHIEVE PHYSICAL INTIMACY IS PROMISE AND POTENTIAL

A *man with promise* is someone who has a destiny and purpose inside of him. If God made a promise to him, then he is just and faithful to do what he promised. When someone has a promise from God, it means that someday this promise will be fulfilled. Promise sparks hope, faith, truth, revelation, and gives light to your darkest situation. Someone standing on a promise is more important than having a plan because a promise suggests **it will happen** and a plan suggests **it might happen**. A man with a promise is icing on the cake for a woman because she will support and stand beside a man with promise since she knows that one day, God will fulfill it.

A *promise* is something you can put your faith and trust in. A *promise* is a binding agreement, meaning it is not meant to be broken. It is also a vow or covenant one makes. When God makes a promise to you, then he is obligated to fulfill that promise because God's Word will not come back void. In other words, God cannot lie.

Promise is a binding agreement or covenant that God never breaks. He always keeps his promises.

Romans 4:16 reads, *"Therefore it is of faith that it might be according to grace, so that the promise might be sure to all the seed."* In this scripture, the promise refers to the promise Jesus made to Abraham that he would make him a father of many nations and make his descendants as the sand of the sea, which cannot be numbered. Therefore, God fulfilled this promise to Abraham as we are the seeds of Abraham.

A man with potential is also important in developing intimacy because he will make his goals happen. Just because he is not there yet, does not mean he won't get there. His future spouse will help him get to where he needs to be. This is so important in achieving intimacy in your relationships because potential does not suggest what is behind you, but what is ahead. It allows you to look past the now and focus on what is to be. What drive, motivation, passion, desire, intensity, or act of desperation do you see inside your man? What are his goals, dreams, and future accomplishments? These things let the women know that he is going somewhere and we definitely don't mind going with him for the ride. A woman will ride with a man even if she doesn't know the destination, but she can see his potential. She will ride it out with him when she sees something in him that lets her know how determined he is. He may not be there yet, but as long as we can see him going somewhere is what is important to us.

A woman will stand by a man who has potential because she sees greatness inside of him.

Many times women fail to look at the potential; instead we concentrate too much on the failures. You cannot keep looking back and expect to press forward. We should only look back for two reasons: to remember how far we have come and to thank God for bringing us to where we are now. Too much time is wasted focusing on what used to be that we fail to look at what could be. I believe so many relationships have lost intimacy because we keep focusing on things in the past such as what he did wrong, what he didn't do, what he said, and so forth. Kirk Franklin wrote a song entitled, *Let It Go*, where it talks about letting go of your past and looking to the future. Let it go and move on. Don't hold onto it because if you do, you will be the one who will suffer the most, not the person who hurt you. Being able to forgive is more for you than it is for the person who hurt you. You have to free yourself from that weight and if not, it will wear you down. Stop carrying unnecessary weight. Even Southwest Airlines knows that too much weight can destroy you. That's why their policy is that you can only carry two small bags on the plane with you and the rest of it goes underneath the aircraft. Too much baggage can risk the plane going down and if that happens, you will die. God wants you to live. Drop that unnecessary weight and move on.

If you are going to achieve the level of intimacy that we have talked about in this book, then you will have to stop focusing on the failures and start looking at the possibilities. Here's a prime example of what happens when we look back when we should be looking ahead. In *Genesis 19*, it discusses about Lot and his wife, who had to get out of the city called Sodom quickly because God had given His Word that He was going to destroy Sodom and everyone there because of the sins of the people. Lot was a wealthy man. He had money and owned wealthy possessions, but God told him to flee with his family to another city and not look back. God said keep going because he did not want them to focus on what they were leaving behind, but instead look towards their future. The Bible states in

Genesis 19:26 that Lot's wife looked back and was turned to a pillar of salt. He taught her a lesson not to look back on what they left behind, but look forward to what is ahead. What we have ahead of us is far greater than what we had five years ago.

> God lives in the future so He can't bless you if you keep looking back.

All of these principles require each of you to put some thought and consideration in your relationships because I believe you are not doing it enough. Put more concentration towards the mental and spiritual principles that I am giving you. You will see the difference. These principles will help you become closer to one another. If the man lacks drive, motivation, and the potential to do better, this may not be the person you should be associated with. Again, know what type of man you are involved with and these principles will help you see what you have now is worth it, or if he needs to be kicked to the curb.

Let's Stay Together by having a Man with Promise and Potential

1. Does your significant other frequently discuss his goals and dreams? What expectations has he put in place to achieve his goals in the near future? Furthermore, do you know what his dreams and aspirations are?

2. What is it about your significant other that shows he has promise and potential in his life? Is it something he does, what he says, or is it his drive or passion towards a specific goal of which indicates that he has potential in achieving what he is passionate about?

3. A promise is something that is concrete and solid. It indicates something that will happen, whereas potential is what could possibly happen. If you have or had someone in your life that lacked promise, but had the potential, would you take a chance on this person? Why or why not?

ELEVENTH AND FINAL KEY TO ACHIEVE PHYSICAL INTIMACY IS THE MAN'S PLACE OF POSITION AND LEADERSHIP

Lastly, the most important key is to have a man who is in his rightful place to be in position for leadership because this is the foundation of the relationship. We expect a man to be in his rightful position or in a place of leadership to be head of the household. This concept is not new. Originally, when God first created man, he gave him dominion over everything in the earth. Therefore, a man who is in his rightful position should possess the qualities to be a leader and the head of your house. If he is not fit to lead, then he is not fit to be the head. You have to know your mate's qualities, characteristics, and behaviors to see if he is fit to lead over you before marriage. Otherwise, you will have an extremely difficult time in making the relationship work because it is not built on a solid foundation.

> If a man is not fit to lead, then he is not fit to lead over you in marriage.

Women are required to submit under the authority and leadership of their husbands. It is a biblical principle required of us. Moreover, a man of God, whom God has chosen for the woman, operates in his rightful place. You will rarely find a man who doesn't want to be the head of the house because it is in him to do so. God created man with the skills, intelligence, and leadership capabilities. What he needs is also integrity, dignity, morals, standards, and to have a relationship with God.

Leadership Characteristics and Qualities:
1. A man who **prays**
2. A man who **praises**
3. **Planner** and **preparer**
4. A man with **promise** and **potential**
5. **Provider**
6. **Protector**
7. A man with **passion**
8. **Performer**
9. **Producer**
10. **Participator**
11. A man with **position** and **leadership**

When a man possesses all these qualities, a woman will have no problem submitting under a godly man of excellence. We are under his leading. However, some men are not capable of leading and do not possess these eleven characteristics listed and discussed throughout this book.

Before you can lead someone else, you have to first learn how to follow. God gave Adam dominion over the earth before he gave him direction, not to eat the forbidden fruit. So, Adam led before he learned to follow, which was the cause of his downfall. When Adam failed to follow God's rules, God threw him out of the Garden of Eden. Even though he was not fit to remain in the garden, God did not disqualify him or take away his leadership roles. He still had dominion, but he just made it a little more difficult for him to get to where he needed to be. *See Genesis 2.*

Who a man is following will determine what type of leader he will be. Check to see who the man in your life is following.

Okay, go back and take a closer look at the principles we have talked about in this book and decide if you have a leader or a follower. Men are governed to lead. Women are destined to follow. Men, I am strictly speaking on leading your household, not your job. Just because you are president of a major corporation doesn't mean you know how to lead your household. How you operate in your business is totally different than how you operate and perform in your home. I am not going to go deep into this, but just know that there is a difference in both and just because you are a great manager on your job doesn't mean you have the qualities to lead a home. When leading a household, you have a wife, children, financial obligations, spiritual considerations, extended family and so much more that you have to deal with and you deal with your family differently than those whom you deal with at work. Family is family and work is work. Let me put it this way: a job is what provides and a family is what sustains. When you lose the job, the family will still be there. You lead your household out of love, respect, and care for the members of your household. However, many people lead their job because of obligation and necessity. For the family, you operate out of love, and for your job, you operate out of obligation and responsibility. It really is that simple. A woman has to know the difference in the two and be aware of what type of leadership man she has: a household leader or a job leader.

> A job is what provides and a family is what sustains.

This principle was meant to be last because all the others preceding were the basis of what this encompasses. I hope you have been taking notes and answering the thought provoking questions at the end of each chapter so you can discuss these things openly and honestly with your husband or your future spouse today, and pray about these things to discover where the two of you are in your relationship. I believe if you follow these basic principles and put them into practice, then the emotional and spiritual intimacy will not be the same in your relationship. It will be stronger and it will tighten the bond in your relationship. The stronger the bond is between couples, the harder for this bond to be broken.

MAIN INGREDIENT IN ACHIEVING THE ELEVEN KEYS

Of all the keys we've talked about in this book, there's still one more that is the most important of all the keys, and without it, your relationship will not withstand. Even if your mate possesses all eleven keys, if he does not practice this one main ingredient, everything else will be miniscule. You will never achieve physical, emotional, or spiritual connection with your spouse without **love** being at the forefront of your relationship. *1 Corinthians 13: 4-7* reads, *"Love suffers long and is kind; love does not envy; love does not parade itself, is not puffed up; does not behave rudely, does not seek its own, is not provoked, thinks no evil; does not rejoice in iniquity, but rejoices in the truth; bears all things, believes all things, hopes all things, endures all things. Love never fails."*

We are not perfect. Therefore, sometimes love can cause pain and hurtful feelings toward another person because she's been hurt. However, if a man loves you, he will ask for your forgiveness and repent for his wrongful actions.

Love means that your husband or mate is not threatened by your success or your calling. He will help you get to where you need to be. He sees your God-given talents and will help you accomplish your destined goals. He will cheer you towards completing your destiny and push you toward excellence to have a fulfilled life. He is not jealous or envious of you, but really supports you in all you do and acts as your cheerleader to help you do what it is you desire to do.

(Remember, a man who is a freeloader does the opposite) Love also means that he will hang in there with you through the rough and trying times and will not leave you, no matter how bad it gets. He is willing to hang in there with you until things get better. Love endures for the long stretch, so he doesn't mind waiting until things get better. Love ensures he doesn't walk away, but believes in doing everything possible to work things out for the best. When one easily quits and gives up, it is a clear sign of the absence of love.

Love never fails.

Love is like glue: hard to remove and when you try to remove, it always leaves a stain where you will know that love once abided there. Love is contagious and transferable; it is like a magnet that attracts people to you, even if those people don't approve of you. It is your force of love that propels them in your direction.

Lastly, part of loving someone else is having trust in that person. Love is honest and genuine. If your husband or significant other isn't truthful, then love is absent. A relationship is built on trust and if your mate can't trust you, then the relationship is already on a downhill slope. A wife needs to trust that her husband will be there for her and trust that he will protect her and be her backbone. She needs to believe he will stick to what he said he would do because his word is his bond. Moreover, she needs to trust that he will take care of the problem or issue when it arises in the home and be able to resolve any conflict. If she can't trust him to provide, support, and protect her, then they will encounter many problems in the relationship that will be difficult to resolve.

Love makes the woman want to please her man. She wants to see him happy because she enjoys doing things to make him happy such as cooking dinner, giving him a massage, rubbing his feet, and surprising him with a soft, sensual and relaxing bubble bath with candles. This form of expression shows him how much she loves, appreciates, and values him. Moreover, it is about giving, not taking when you love someone. You thrive to see his happiness before your own and he'll do the same for you; reciprocal of love.

Ladies, think about what you would do if you no longer have him in your life and if he wasn't around anymore. Think about what your life would be like without him. Would you be miserable, sad, lonely, unhappy, and empty? If your answer is yes, then clearly this means your relationship is filled with love and affection. If your answer is no, then your relationship does not contain love. Maybe you got involved for all the wrong or right reasons such as he was a nice person, but whatever your reasons were, love was not part of the equation.

> Whatever your reasons were to get involved with him, if love was not the dominating factor, the relationship won't last.

Married ladies do this: Watch your husband sleep for a little while. When you get out of bed for work or when he sleeps in late on the weekend, watch him, and concentrate on what your life would be like without him. As you observe his mannerisms, think about how you are feeling right now. Think about all the wonderful things he did, and the things he does that get on your nerves, how he makes you laugh, and how much fun you have together, and so forth. As you think about all these things that have occurred in the relationship, then hopefully, you will see the good more than the bad in your marriage. If you have trouble thinking of anything, then it may be an indication that there is no love because a person who loves someone can easily think about all the reasons why you love this person. Maybe the love is there, but you haven't shown it towards the other person in a while and you've forgotten what was really important to you. If you love him, then an abundance of memories will flood through your mind that may even put a smile on your face as you are reading this. This indicates you love him. Finally, when was the last time you told him, "I love you?" Was it a few days ago, a few months ago, last year for Christmas, last year on your birthday, or some other important event or day? Think about it. If it was a while ago, then begin implementing today by showing consistent reminders of your love, appreciation, and affection for him.

Ephesians 5:25 reads, *"Husbands, love your wives, just as Christ also loved the church and gave himself for her."* Christ loved us so much that he died for us. He was determined that he would die for us rather than live without us and this is how Christ instructs husbands to love their wives. Husbands must protect, provide, pray for her, comfort, cover her, listen and pay attention to her words, meet her needs and desires and be there for her, period. Husbands must cherish their wives like Christ does the church. Husbands should love their wives as they love and take care of themselves. Paul admonishes in the book of Ephesians that wives are to submit to their husbands, which means wives are to respect their husbands as the leading authority under God's covering in the household. It is important to note that wives are not directed to love their husbands, but directed to submit to them because of the importance of submitting to their husband's leadership. Just like God gave Adam dominion over the Garden of Eden in the book of Genesis is similar to what Paul is addressing in the book of Ephesians. Men are leaders and were originally designed to be in positions of authority as God orchestrated in the beginning of creation. Therefore, it is important that wives submit to their husbands as God ordained. Men operate best as leaders and women operate best as assistants or helpmates.

> Husbands love your wives and wives submit to your husbands.

In the Garden of Eden, Adam submitted to his wife Eve's request, and they sinned by eating the forbidden fruit that God told Adam not to eat. Now, God wants us to correct this error, and wives are to follow their husbands and the husbands are to follow God. God is allowing us to get our marriages in line with His will because man sinned against God after submitting to the woman and lost focus on God's divine order of things. Again, the wife is to submit to her husband and not the other way around.

When we do things contrary to God's will, our relationships will suffer. Some of your marriages are falling apart because of power issues: the wife refuses to submit to her husband and the husband refuses to submit to God. Each person does what is right in his own eyes and this brings about chaos and disorder. God gave Adam dominion. Adam was to listen and obey God, but instead, he disobeyed God's command to not eat from the forbidden tree and instead listened to the woman, where things went terribly wrong.

Your marriage should resemble this:

God leads the husband so the wife can be in position to follow her spouse. Then, both are following God's direction, guidance, and will. The husband steps into his leadership role to follow God and seek Him to be the head over his household and family. The wife still has her own personal relationship with God, but she follows her husband's lead as the head of the household.
↑

Husband follows God. Husband prays, meditates on God's word, fasts, and seeks God's direction in the marriage. The husband listens and obeys God's instructions. In turn, the wife listens and submits to her husband's authority because she knows he's listening and following God. She also sees he has an intimate relationship with God.
↑

Woman follows her husband's leading also known as the head of the household.

Notice that the arrows are going up because God is the head and leader in our lives. He is a sovereign God. What He says goes. Period! If you follow Him, you will never, ever go wrong. The problem is we don't follow Him. If the husband doesn't follow God, the wife will have a difficult time following God too. He is not following God's proper chain of command and then the relationship falls apart and is in disarray. If you operate your marriage with God in it, your marriage will not be easily broken. Remember, this was the eleventh key we talked about in this book. It is vital to your relationship if you have the proper covering.

Here are a few examples of husbands in the Bible who displayed their leading in a marriage in a godly manner and wives submitted to their husband's authority. The Bible records in Exodus 4 that Moses took his wife and his sons with him after God spoke to him through a burning bush to lead the Israelites out of enslavement. God spoke to Moses and the wife followed. Another example is when Joseph was warned in a dream by an angel that King Herod was seeking to destroy baby Jesus. The angel told him not to return to King Herod, but to flee to Egypt. Joseph obeyed and took his wife, Mary, and baby Jesus to Egypt. Again, we see here that the Word of God came to the husband and the wife submitted to his authority. This is found in Matthew 1:18-23. Lastly, in Genesis 12:1-5, God told Abram to leave his country and his family to travel to a foreign land that He will show him. God also promised to make his name great among the descendants and a father of many nations. Abram took his wife, Sarai, with him on this journey. God spoke again to the husband and the wife followed.

In the Bible, we see many times where God spoke to the husband and the wife submitted to her husband's leadership. If your husband gets a vision from God to move to another state to pastor a church and he gets clear direction and insight from God, then the wife must submit to her husband and go with him. It is okay to pray together and seek confirmation from God. Sometimes, He may confirm His Word to both of them. At other times, He may not, so the wife has to trust her husband's leadership and know that he heard from God. God desires for the wife to trust and have confidence in her husband's decisions. He can choose not to share or confirm anything with her. Know your husband's spiritual relationship with God, as having an intimate relationship with God signifies that he is able to discern God's voice in order to be obedient to His Word. If he listens and obeys God's direction, then the wife will have no problem listening and following after his leadership because he seeks after God's own heart.

> If God speaks to the husband and the husband follows God, then the wife's duty is to follow the husband because he is following God. Please be sure you know who your husband is following.

A husband excels and thrives off his wife's admiration for him. She admires and respects his leadership abilities, decisions and choices. In addition, the wife can offer advice and input where necessary and the husband should value her input and opinion, but for the success of the home, she relies on the husband. Again, you have to verify your husband's leadership abilities and godly qualities that indicate if he is fit to lead the household. Review the eleven keys previously discussed and apply immediately.

A wife should not belittle, downgrade, or insult her husband because it's disrespectful and brings him dishonor. He will have a difficult time in leading and performing effectively in his God-given ability to lead. The same authority and ability that God gave Adam to lead is the same ability that every man possesses, but hasn't tapped into yet. Maybe he got distracted by a beautiful woman like Adam and David when they both fell at the hands of a woman. Adam fell because of Eve and David fell because of Bathsheba. Or maybe he got distracted by power and money, and turned his attention on those things instead of God like King Nebuchadnezzar. Once he realizes who he is in Christ

Jesus, his entire outlook will change and he will see himself as a leader and role model. Leaders lead from the front and not the back.

If a man does not receive respect from his wife, he will look for it elsewhere, whether it is drugs, alcohol, sex, or other people. The main reasons a person joins a gang are to receive respect and to have a sense of belonging. Here is a prime example in the Bible on how men view respect. This book is rarely ever talked about or preached about in churches, but is a resourceful and great story on respect and authority. In Esther 1, Queen Vashti disobeys her husband, King Ahasuerus's request. The King becomes furious, angry, humiliated, and upset after she does not follow his direct order. He calls for his wife, for all his friends and kingdom to see her beauty before them. She refuses to be showcased as his trophy. Then, he holds a banquet after her dishonor and not respecting his request by replacing her role as a queen with a new queen, which was Esther. Remember, what I told you earlier that men will get respect elsewhere if you don't give it to them. The king's former wife, Queen Vashti, disrespects his authority and position. She fails to acknowledge, honor his wishes, and give him special attention. Can you imagine how this made the king feel and how it made him look in front of others? He is the king and he can't have a wife who disrespects and fails to acknowledge his authority and position. The king's reasoning is that if all of the other husbands' wives learn of the queen's behavior, she will set a bad example for other women, so he removed her from the kingdom.

The husband desires and needs respect from his wife because it affirms his value and worth as a leader in the home.

Respect for your husband affirms his value, power, and self-worth. When his wife respects him at home, she will also respect him in public. When you display a high regard for your man, it also demonstrates how much "swag" he has. He will have moments where he can upset you and you disagree with his actions because no one is perfect, but a wife should stand by him and support his decisions and ideas, even when he makes a mistake. She should still uphold him and stroke his ego by cheering him on because he will perform better with his cheerleader in his corner. Cheerleaders help the players win games.

For further explanation on the *value of respect*, let's examine two people in the Bible who suffered from the consequences of being disrespectful and refused to esteem the man of God. In Numbers 12, Miriam questions Moses' authority and leadership because of his choice to marry an Ethiopian woman. Miriam also questions whether Moses' decision is lead by God. Miriam's reaction to Moses' marital relationship undermines his authoritative position to uphold other manners. She also questions his character. God is upset with Miriam's behavior towards his servant, Moses, and inflicts her body with leprosy for seven days. After seven days, she was made whole again once she acknowledged her dishonoring behavior and repented. Overall, God was displeased with Miriam's questioning the authority and leadership of Moses, whom He selected, appointed, and called during this season. God allows His wrath and judgment to fall on her because she questions the man whom He has put in charge to lead the people out of Israel.

The second example to review is found in Job 2:9, where Job's wife tells him to curse God and die because of all the pain and inflictions that came upon him. *Job 2:9* reads, *"Then his wife said to him, 'Do you still hold fast to your integrity? Curse God and die!'"* His wife tells him to *give up and die*, meaning accept your fate and don't try to persevere and fight through it. She doesn't encourage her own husband to live through it or comfort him through his time of trouble. She tells him to deny the god who created him and who once blessed him, *to just die*, meaning give up on his life. Job's wife should have reminded him of the godly man he was and that prayer can bring him out of his storm and to continue to trust in God to bring him out of his turmoil. Instead, she tells him to curse God and die. Wow! How harsh and cruel is that coming from your own wife who is supposed to support you, comfort you, encourage you, respect you, and most importantly, love you.

Job calls his wife foolish. She has to accept the good along with the bad. Since Job has experienced nothing but good in the earlier years his life, he learns to accept the bad as well because God is still magnificent in His majesty and power. Now, the Bible never mentions Job's wife after this chapter, so we don't know whether she was still living when God restored everything back to Job. Overall, Job's wife disrespects him with her crucial remarks and she becomes insignificant because she's never mentioned again. Actually, her name is never mentioned in the book of Job. Moreover, insignificant people cannot affect your God-given talents and calling.

Above all the eleven keys mentioned in this book, your relationship must contain love, and if you love him, you will respect him as the head of your household as God ordained him to be. Again, if your mate possesses these eleven keys, then that is a definite indication that he is fit to lead. Let love continue to abound in your relationship and continue to follow the proper ordinance of God's law as indicated prior where wives submit to their husbands, and husbands submit to God. When you do this, both of you are following God because the husband is seeking Him.

Know what leadership really means to you and to God- husband operating in the home as the head of the household and the wife submitting to his authority. If he is not fit to lead, he is not fit to lead over you in marriage. I hope each of you assess your relationship and examine each of the eleven keys. Additionally, ponder on the thought-provoking questions posed in each chapter for further discussion with your mate. If you do all of these things, you will be on a successful path of a great, long-lasting relationship with meaningful love for each other, love for Christ Jesus, and a love for others.

> *Leadership in the home* means the husband is operating as head of the household and the wife is submitting to his authority.

After giving you the eleven principles towards achieving physical intimacy in your relationships, we still haven't applied any of them yet. I will dissect each principle by using a biblical character, Job, from the Bible. We will also discuss the ways in which he embodies all eleven principles. As we go through each of these, start thinking about how you can begin implementing these in your relationship now. God led me to read and review Job's story again. Although many of us have read the book of Job many times before, but each time you see something different and gain new revelation. Again, I have learned so much from reading about Job. Let's review the book of Job.

Let's Stay Together by Having a Man who is a Leader

1. Does your significant other meet his leadership roles in your household? What qualities or characteristics does he demonstrate that he is a leader and not a follower?

2. Review the leadership qualities highlighted in this chapter and were outlined in this book. Does your significant other encompass these qualities? If he does not have all of these, make a list of the ones he does not possess as a leader. How can he improve on those you listed?

3. All eleven principles are necessary to have a successful relationship or marriage, yet some more necessary than others, name the characteristics that are most needed and why. After you choose the characteristics that your significant other needs to possess, does he possess these characteristics and if not, why did you decide to be with someone who did not possess the necessary traits to win your affection?

APPLYING THE ELEVEN PRINCIPLES TO JOB'S LIFE

1. *Prayer (Job 1:5)*: Job offered burnt offerings to the Lord on behalf of his children in case they had sinned and cursed God. Job prayed for his friends. Later, God restored all that was lost to Job after he interceded for someone else (*Job 42:10*). When Job interceded for someone else, God, in turn, opened doors on his behalf. God didn't bless Job until after he prayed for others.

2. *Praise (Job 1:20-22)*: Job praised God even after he lost his money and his family. The Scripture reads, *"And he fell to the ground and worshipped. And he said: naked I came from my mothers' womb, and naked shall I return there. The Lord gave, and the Lord has taken away; Blessed be the name of the Lord."*

3. *Plan (Job 3:25)*: Job was a wealthy and prosperous man. God blessed his entire household. Job prayed for his children and he planned to leave an inheritance for each of them. Job's plans got interrupted when God allowed Satan to attack his money, family, and his health. Job states that what he greatly feared has now come on him. He dreaded this day coming, but he knew it was going to come one day. He had a plan, but he didn't know that God had bigger plans for him than he had for himself. At least, Job had a plan. God changed Job's plan because He had one.

4. *Performance (Job 1):* Job was blameless and upright before the Lord. He feared God and did not partake of evil things. He was a just and righteous man.

5. *Protection (Job 1:10):* God put a shield of protection around Job and blessed all he had. God allowed Satan to test Job's faithfulness towards him. In other words, Satan had to be given permission from God to do anything to His elect. Therefore, Satan could not do anything to Job without God's permission.

6. *Production (Job 1:3):* Job produced results because of the way he lived and served God. Everything Job touched, God blessed. He was known as the greatest of the people in the land. Job's possessions were 7,000 sheep, 3,000 camels, 500 oxen, 500 donkeys, and an enormous household.

7. *Passion (Job 27:3-6):* Job continued to be passionate about serving and living holy for God even after his loss. He refused to turn away from God. The Scripture reads, *"As long as breath is in me, and the breath of God in my nostrils, my lips will not speak wickedness, nor my tongue utter deceit." Verse 6: "My righteousness I hold fast, and will not let it go."*

8. *Participation (Job 42:3):* Job confessed his faults and repented to God. He thought God had dealt with him unjustly and had judged him harshly. Moreover, he thought God had forsaken him. He repented to God and confessed for misjudging God, for he sees God in a different light. He knew that God was awesome, just, and divine and His majesty rules the earth.

9. *Providing (Job 42:11):* God gave Job double for his trouble. Job continued to provide for his children. He was still able to leave an inheritance for them once God restored all that he had lost.

10. *Promise and Potential (Job 42:12):* God blessed the latter days of Job more than his beginning. Job lived 140 years, where he saw his children and grandchildren of four generations. Job died wealthy with an abundance of prosperity where he left a legacy after he passed.

11. *Position and Place of Leadership (Job 1:1-10):* Job's position was that he was blessed. He lived righteously and unselfishly. He was rich and owned great possessions, where he was known as the greatest in the land. Job set an example for others to follow. Even his friends couldn't figure him out. They judged and condemned him because of the adversity he faced, but they didn't know God's hands were on Job through it all. Job displayed leadership because he confessed his sins and repented to God for doubting him. He also prayed for his friends' deliverance too. This displayed what type of man Job truly was, because his friends betrayed him while Job still remained faithful to God.

Didn't I tell you that these simple, basic keys are obtainable? Every man needs to possess these principles. Now is the time to check your potential mate to see if he is qualified or disqualified, and wait on the man that God will qualify to be your husband.

We have talked about what intimacy means, what intimacy does, how it makes you feel, and finally how to achieve intimacy in your relationships by applying the eleven principles. We have even dissected Job's life of which came from the Bible and applied the eleven keys. However, I feel that this book would not be complete without applying practical, real life applications, aside from the Bible. It is one thing to discuss these things and what to look for, but what makes it real and obtainable is when you apply these eleven keys in your relationships.

How will you achieve all the principles I just gave you? How do you implement these things when you are in a relationship? What are the things you need to do to sustain your relationship? I know some of you are thinking to yourselves that these eleven keys are only applicable for those who are unmarried, but what about those who are already married? Where do you go from here now that you are married and your marriage is rocky or shaky? You also acknowledge that your spouse lacks the ability to produce, praise, perform, participate, plan, or pray. You can still use these eleven principles in your marriage whether or not your spouse possesses them. These are things that you can still work on together or individually. Some of these will require both of you to take a self-examination to see where you are and where you want to be.

Moreover, I found a way to help married couples by giving you real life situations from my siblings, who are married, and some are divorced, to help you get your relationship in order. I have twelve brothers and sisters and three of them have been through various trials with their spouses. Therefore, they are sharing some things that occurred in their relationships that hopefully will help you achieve intimacy in yours. Before I get to the heart of the discussions, where three of my siblings share their stories, I just want to give all the married couples some solid pointers to apply in your relationships today that will point you in the direction of achieving a greater level of intimacy. Married couples, thank you all for sticking with me this long. I told you I had something for you too and I know you all were also helped in these eleven keys. These six simple things you can do today that will help you begin achieving a greater depth of intimacy in your relationship. **These are for married couples only**.

Before the Lights Go Out: Applying the Eleven Principles to Job's Life

1. We have applied all eleven principles to Job's life. What other person in the Bible would you apply the eleven principles too? Write specific examples on how the eleven principles apply to this person from the Bible.

2. Why was it so important for Job to pray for his friends before he received his blessing? What lesson was God giving Job by telling him to pray for his friends, those same friends who doubted him, ridiculed him, and scorned him?

3. On the discussion topic outlining the principle of planning for Job's life, what was Job's plan? Do you think God would have interrupted Job's plan if he didn't have one? In other words, would God have moved in Job's life the way he did if Job didn't have a plan for his life?

SIX SIMPLE THINGS TO INCREASE INTIMACY IN YOUR MARRIAGE

1. Take walks together

The first thing you can do to increase intimacy in your marriage is to take regular walks together, whether in your neighborhood or in the park. Not only does walking relieve stress and tension, it is also a good way to converse and resolve conflicts. Recently, I was talking with one of my best friends and she stated that she walks in the park with her husband to resolve tension and disputes. Rather than yelling, screaming, or throwing objects at one another, they leave their environment of tension and stress to step into a place of peace and tranquility. She also admitted that she refuses to argue in her bedroom because her bedroom is a place of her refuge and solidarity. She reads, listens to music, watches television, does her homework, sleeps, and makes love to her husband—all these activities are done in her bedroom. Don't contaminate your sacred space with tension and arguments.

> Guard your sacred space away from tension, strife and stress, and fill it with peace, solace, comfort, and tranquility.

When you are overwhelmed with stress, it can be harder to see things clearly. Once you get out of the mess you are in, the situation will become clearer to you, where you are able to think logically on a greater level of consciousness towards the situation. This is excellent advice for married couples because there will be times when you and your spouse will not agree on everything. So, you need to be able to talk sensibly about the issues, without yelling and screaming. Sometimes, you need to get away to calm down and speak peaceably about the problems. Singer, actress, and songwriter Jill Scott released a song a few years ago entitled *A Long Walk*. In the song, she sings about taking a walk in the park and sitting down conversing with the person you are dating. Additionally, Jill Scott sings in her song that a long walk will give you relaxation, stimulation, conversation, education, and so forth. A long walk is also a song about developing intimacy. Taking a long walk invokes effective communication, improves your listening skills, while it allows you to be open and honest with the other person. This is a place to be in a peaceful, relaxing environment. What is a better way to get to know someone else than by taking a walk in the park? Moreover, this is great advice from Jill Scott. Married couples need to get a copy of the Jill Scott CD, *Who is Jill Scott?* to listen to the words, and see where she is coming from.

2. Read books together

The second way of increasing intimacy in your marriage is by reading books together. This is an excellent form of communication and relaxation because reading expands your knowledge and vocabulary and opens a forum for dialogue. If you have nothing else to talk about, then talk about the book and what your feelings are about it. The whole point about reading books together is that both of you read the same book and then have discussions afterwards. You can see each other's viewpoints and discuss things that you would not have otherwise discussed by reading this book together.

The book does not have to be a relationship-related manual. Yet, you can read challenging books that are thought-provoking and evokes a discussion. It's a good idea that you read something he likes and also read something you like, and then discuss the books after you read them. Find time to read and a place where you can discuss the book, and point out things you agree or disagree with. You will see how positive and effective this simple form of communication will have on your relationships.

> Reading books together helps improve communication, helps you relax and allow you to spend quality time together.

You do not have to read only as a hobby, but also read to achieve results, whether it is for relaxation, or spending time with your spouse. As long as the both of you are getting something out of it, then you are achieving something worthwhile and meaningful.

3. Have date nights

The third way of increasing intimacy in your marriage is by dating regularly. Dating is so important in achieving and sustaining intimacy in your marriage. Married couples I can not stress this enough that in order to have a long-lasting marriage, you have to sustain the intimacy in your marriage. In other words, don't let it die. Please keep the fires burning, even if they are dim and barely lit. As long as there is a little fire, there is spark and hope. We know over time that the fire in your marriage may not be as bright as it was before, but love never dies. Mrs. Michelle Obama did an interview once where she stated that she and her husband, President Barack Obama, had date nights every Friday. Why is this so important? It's important for them to do this so they can stay connected to one another and keep their fire burning. Both of them have extremely busy lives as the demands of a president and raising children can take a negative toil on your marriage if you let it.

With the determination, desire, and dedication to make your marriage work no matter what, there are certain things you have to do to sustain it and to remain connected, not drift apart. You cannot let work or your children drive a wedge between the two of you. You have to draw the line somewhere. Set boundaries to avoid your marriage failing. Otherwise, you will end up alone and raising the children solo while your husband is traveling six days a week. It would be extremely difficult to keep the marriage afloat when you are only seeing your husband one day a week. Not only that, your children only sees their father once a week and he will miss spending quality time with you and the children. Furthermore, he is failing to meet his wife's emotional, physical, and spiritual needs. You need to firmly establish all three to have an intimate relationship. If even one of these qualities is missing in your relationship, you will surely know it because your relationship will begin to crumble.

Don't get so consumed or too busy that you don't make time for your mate because he/she will begin to feel neglected and unimportant and this will cause a big drift in your relationship.

Make sure one of your priorities in your busy schedule includes spending time with family and spending one-on-one quality time with your spouse. Spending quality time with your spouse connects both of you on a deeper, intimate level. Some couples believe that spending quality time is by having sex, and if you think that way, you are missing the mark. Again, we have to take our minds off the physical aspects of the relationship and concentrate more on the spiritual and emotional side. Spending valuable quality time is what one does outside the bedroom such as reading books, taking walks, having date nights, going on vacations, and so on.

All of these things require time and effort and none of these activities involve sexual contact. Again, the more time you spend with someone, the closer you will get to that person and the deeper your feelings will be towards him. It also gives you a greater level of respect and admiration when you realize that there is so much more to the relationship than sex. Think about this: would you love your spouse if you did not have sex with him/her again? If the answer is yes, then your relationship is solid and strong. If the answer is no, then your relationship is mostly built on the physical aspects of the person and may not last. I know sex is very important in a relationship, but it is not entirely what your relationship should be built on. Hopefully, you are beginning to understand this by reading this book to concentrate more on the emotional and spiritual side to gain a greater level of intimacy in your marriage. For many of you reading this book, sex is not keeping you and your mate together nor did it cause you two to fall apart. Ponder that!

4. Think outside of the box and do things in the spur of the moment

The fourth way of increasing intimacy in your marriage is by doing things out of the box, at the spur of the moment, for one another. Some examples are putting a love letter in his briefcase or luggage, or sending flowers or candy as a "just because," not necessarily a holiday, birthday, or anniversary. By doing these simple things, you let him know that you are thinking about him/her and how much you love him/her.

Remember, those good old-fashioned love letters that we use to write to the boys we liked during our elementary years because we were too shy to tell him. Not only will it be memorable, romantic, and spontaneous, it is also a heartfelt and meaningful tool that came from you. It is not another Hallmark card (I'm not knocking Hallmark), but it's coming from the heart from the one who loves him dearly. You can also take a half of day off from work to surprise him with a picnic lunch, or a walk on the beach or park, or even take an early lunch to go see a movie. Moreover, you don't have to spend a lot of money to have fun. All you need is time and a little creativity, and he will absolutely love it. He will love it even more when you think about doing special things for him because it means that you put some thought, effort, and consideration into it to spend time with him.

> Spontaneity is fun, exciting, adventurous, and creative—all the things that builds the excitement in your relationship.

Wives, you have no idea how simple things like this mean so much to him because if you knew how much he needed it, then why don't you do it? Husbands, why do the wives have to plan or suggest everything? Sometimes, you need to show a little bit of thoughtfulness and creativity by doing special things for them too. It does not have to be her birthday or holiday to express your love with gifts and go on dates, but because you are thinking about her. Therefore, start implementing and planning special dates to be with the woman you love. You will receive rewarding results afterwards. If you do these special dates occasionally, you will see a profound, positive difference in your relationships. Additionally, your love-making will be "off the chain."

5. Spend time with your mate's extended family

The fifth way of increasing intimacy in your marriage is by spending time with your extended family. In other words, spending time with his family and yours will greatly improve the intimacy in your marriage. Not only does spending time with each other's families offer a greater depth of understanding and wisdom of each other backgrounds and family history, it will also improve relations between both families. If you want a close-knit family and marriage, this is what is needed to learn about your immediate families to see how you can work with your mate. How can you say you love me, but hate my family, when my family is a part of who I am?

There are so many people who cannot get along with their in-laws or extended families; it affects their marriage. This will affect your relationship with your spouse because the two families can't get along with each other. Now, maybe you can deal with him not getting along with your siblings, but not getting along with your parents is another issue since they are the ones who raised you. Therefore, if he does not like them, then it makes you wonder what his true feelings are about you. Does he really like you? *1 John 4:21* reads, *"If someone says, "I love God," and hates his brother, he is a liar; for he who does not love his brother whom he has seen, how can he love God whom he has not seen?"*

If you do not respect or love your in-laws shows that you do not love God. This is what this scripture is saying. No way can you say you love God and hate your family, because God is love. If you don't love God, it is possible that you would not love your extended family or in-laws because the love of God is not in you. Experience God's love and you will find it easier to connect with your in-laws and appreciate each other's heritage or culture. You will see things that you never knew about each other.

> Your family is an extension of who you are and your spouse's family is an extension of who he is. It is vital to your relationship that you spend time with both sides so you can have a greater level of understanding of who your spouse really is.

Now, let me clear this one thing up: there is a huge difference between liking and loving. You can dislike someone and still love him. God dislikes some of the choices we make, but still loves us. *Romans 5: 8* states, *"But God demonstrates his own love toward us, in that while we were still sinners, Christ died for us."* This demonstrates God's unconditional and limitless love for us in that He loves us despite our faults, failures, issues, problems, and disruptive behaviors. So, you don't necessarily have to like your extended family members, but you do have to love them. *Liking* refers to how you feel towards a particular person or thing whether you agree or not; whereas *loving* refers to having a strong attachment, devotion, or affection for someone. *Love* is deep, intense, and intimate. *Love* is tender, warm, gentle, and authentic. It goes beyond the surface of a mutual liking or disagreement. For example, a person may not like your clothes or your shoes, but still loves you because of the warmth and kind feelings he feels for you despite what you're wearing. So, since God is love, we must demonstrate His love in us by showing it outwardly towards others.

A family that prays together will surely stay together. This is a proven statement. I am a witness to this notion, for my family has been able to stay together all this time by trusting God for His promises through prayer. You will later learn more about my three siblings on how their marriages survived.

6. Go on vacations

The sixth way of applying intimacy in your marriage is by taking vacations together. Get away. When you leave your home, you will spend "real" quality time together because your mind is not on your surroundings, but focused on each other. You are leaving your issues, problems, circumstances, and situations at home. You are enjoying each other while on vacation and falling in love with your spouse all over again.

If you are having problems in your marriage and there is a lot of tension and stress and you two just can't seem to get along anymore, then it may be time to take a quick weekend vacation to take your mind off your problems. Your problems will not erase, but will be much easier to deal with once you return back home. A little bit of rest and relaxation makes a huge difference in how you resolve conflicts. Rest and relaxation is healthy for your body, mind, and spirit. You will be more focused and calmer, thus allowing you to think objectively when you approach your problems.

On this special trip, you will focus on what makes your relationship work because when you focus on the good side of the relationship, dealing with the bad side will be much easier to deal with. You will have a greater chance of working your issues out before returning home.

> Focusing on the good and healthy parts of the marriage will help you become better equipped to handle the issues and problems.

You do not have to leave your home to find relaxation, but getting away a few times a year will surely expand the level of intimacy in your marriage. You do not have to take an island vacation such as Jamaica or Virgin Islands to get away. Instead, you can take a two-hour drive to a resort and make love all day and night long, without distractions or interruptions. I'm sure that there's not a single person on this planet that doesn't enjoy sex. Well, maybe one or two. So, have fun and enjoy what God made to be a beautiful wonderful experience between a husband and wife. Hey, if you don't want to take advantage of the gift of sex, then please pray for your sista here who's still waiting for her husband and who's been waiting for quite some time.

Before Adam and Eve sinned by eating the forbidden fruit, God gave them everything they needed or could ever want. The only requirement was obedience. Adam and Eve could make love all day long if they wanted to. After all, they were married. Like I stated earlier, eating the forbidden fruit opened up their eyes to see what God wasn't ready for them to see yet. He was trying to develop and mature them first, but they got curious and anxious, and decided not to wait on God. Their blessings in disguise was sex, but the curse for Eve was the pain in bearing children and for Adam, tilling the ground or labor to eat, which was the result of their disobedience.

God made sex to be enjoyable, meaningful and fun, but only for those who are married. *Marriage* is a covenant shared with two people under God. Why? Because of the sacredness and sanctity of marriage, we have to be careful and selective with whom we sleep with. (Remember, we discussed earlier about the woman receiving from the man.) Married couples have the right to enjoy each other's company, unwind, and have pleasurable sex. It's in God's will and plan for you, so it's okay to enjoy sex. Besides this, your marriage will be healthy and strong when you have the emotional, physical, and spiritual connection in line. Remember, you need all three. Otherwise, you will not have a successful marriage without all of them.

Now is a good time to talk about my siblings who have had some major problems in their marriages, but despite the issues, they were able to stay together. Their names have not been changed, so these are their real-life actual names.

Sometimes, God will use people in your circle. I have also found that you don't have to go looking for things. God will bring what you need, as He did for me. Moreover, I hope you are blessed by my family's personal testimonies as they speak openly and honestly about their marriages. In the case studies, I have asked each of them specific questions so we could address those things that will help you in your marriages. It will also shed light on what intimacy is about for those of you who still need more insight on this topic.

Before the Lights Go Out: Six Simple Things to Increase Intimacy

1. What types of activities are practiced as a couple to increase the intimacy in your marriage?

2. What are some things that keep you from spending quality time with your husband? What are you going to change to ensure that you will continue to do these things for each other in order to keep your marriage healthy and strong?

3. Aside from the birthdays, special holidays, and anniversaries, what are some things that your spouse does in the spur of the moment that puts a smile on your face?

CASE STUDY #1:

Marlena (sister) and Andrew Lewis (brother-in-law) have been married for ten years, and are in their mid-thirties.

Question: How do you resolve conflicts? What are some methods that you use to keep you from yelling or screaming in front of your child to avoid your child being affected by you and your husband's disagreements? When you need to discuss something and your child is present, what do you do?

Marlena's Response: Andrew and I are not perfect, but one thing we both agree on is not to argue in front of our son, Joshua, who is five years old. If we know that a disagreement is brewing, we will request Joshua to go to his room. After the conversation, we allow Joshua to come downstairs and reassure him that his parents are not mad at him, and tell him that we both love him. Joshua, however, heard a dispute between us. Afterward, we had to explain to him that his parents are just having a disagreement in which is normal in families and the issue has nothing to do with him. Kids see and hear things within the home, but I think that communication is the key. Once you see that the child has been exposed to a disagreement; stop the conversation, and explain to him that it is a normal behavior since parents agree to disagree and his parents still love him.

Author's Perspective: I agree with Marlena's perspective on how you should prevent the child from witnessing an argument between the parents. However, there are times when the child will see the mother and father in a disagreement or argument. What do you do? It is recommended by psychologists that parents should refrain from arguing, yelling or screaming in front of the children because it affects them in so many negative ways. In most cases, the child will begin imitating what they see and hear and begin acting out and doing things contrary to their parents' will.

Children should experience and witness a loving, healthy relationship between two people and see their parents loving one another, and showing affection towards one another such as holding hands, hugging, and/or a peck on the lips or cheek in a tactful, respectful manner. When children see this affection, then they will have an understanding and deeper appreciation for what real love is supposed to look like. It is normal to have discord between two different people, who have an arduous and challenging task of becoming as one in a marriage. At times, it is advised to leave the child in the room so he/she can witness their parents trying to resolve the issue. Let the child know how to resolve conflicts or differences of opinion and how to settle matters so he/she will know what to do if ever placed in that situation.

Therefore, keep all arguments or disagreements between the spouses, but sometimes that child needs to hear what is going on so he/she will understand the issue and also see their parents working towards a resolution. I must add a disclaimer that there are certain things that children shouldn't be exposed to too soon such as sex, but things like the husband forgetting to pick his son or daughter up from daycare can be an example of discussing the issue in front of the child. I must advise parents to use wisdom in what they allow their children to witness.

We don't live in a fairy tale world. Therefore, we have real relationships with real problems and the child needs to hear and understand that. Address those problems head on, talk about the problems openly and honestly with the intent to come to a resolution. Make up in your mind that you are going to work this out so that these disagreements are resolved, where you don't leave the issue still hanging over your head for an extended period of time. Work it out. This will improve the emotional, physical, and spiritual intimacy in your relationship.

CASE STUDY #2:

Burnett (brother) and Dawn Derice Sheppard (sister-in-law) have been married for eleven years, and are in their upper-thirties.

Question: What keeps you and your wife together? In other words, why are staying in the marriage? What are some of the things that keep you from leaving or walking away from your marriage vows? When you consider leaving, you might say, "I can't do this anymore?"

Burnett's Response: We have been married for eleven years. What keeps us together is our willingness to learn from one another through our conversations. To be married is a daily task. Women have so many emotions and if the husband doesn't understand those emotions, he will miss the mark every single time. In our relationship, sex was a huge factor. However, my wife wants to be romanced and I didn't know how to do that. As a man, I figured if I bought her some of the things she desired that this would satisfy the need and leave her smiling, and would also transcend into the bedroom. WRONG! I found out quickly that material items were not the answer. Don't get me wrong, I touched and caressed her daily believing this was romantic. I wasn't that far off; however, I wasn't exactly hitting home runs either.

Derice would tell me exactly what she needed from me as her man, but I wasn't listening. For men, it is an art to listen. One has to practice hearing the words and processing those words into the brain. I was hearing her, but wasn't listening or comprehending.

As we have grown older, our conversations have grown too. We find ourselves agreeing on the same things. However, a few years prior, we would be arguing like animals. We have also grown not only in age, but in marital wisdom. We are telling each other often how much we mean to each other. We say we love each other even more often. Those words need to be said, because they mean something to the one you love. Moreover, love in any relationship can overcome the worst of circumstances. Marriage is a daily fight.

In the Marine Corps, six to thirteen months deployments are common, men have approached Derice and women have approached me too. Trust is another major issue that leads to honesty and security. There will always be issues or situations that arise in our relationship. We both are willing to discuss the topic and make decisions together.

As a man, I am the head of my family, but this head transforms into the Spiritual Head. My wife has to be content with who she is and where she is in her life to comprehend and accept her responsibilities as my wife. I try not to walk ahead of her, but she knows that I am the spiritual leader. Sometimes, this alleviates many arguments. I may not always act as the leader God has called me to be, but we both have acknowledged Jesus as our personal Lord and Savior. This alone makes for both parties to have a mutual understanding and to be submissive to each other's needs.

Derice's Response: From my point of view as the wife, there are many women who need to understand that they set the tone in a marriage. Women have to step back and let the men lead, then they would see their marriages run more smoothly. For an example, when Burnett (Capae) was drinking a lot, I would fuss and yell, and all that did was make him do it more. Once I learned to let God handle him, I stopped fussing and yelling, and shortly later, he stopped drinking. The more a woman fusses, the more he will do what you despise. A woman needs to hold her peace and watch.

The book, *Women are from Venus and Men are from Mars*, I will attest that it is true that men have no clue. Men are like kids, where most of them do not know what they want until we let them know. The best way to handle a man in a marriage goes by the saying that our grandmothers would say, "You will get more bees with honey than with vinegar." With this saying, no one can go wrong.

Author's Perspective: Communication is essential in your relationships because your needs cannot be met if there isn't any effective communication. Not only is communication important, but you both have to listen to each other's desires, needs, and wants and find ways to meet them. I talked about marriage and compromise in my last book, but it is so important that women communicate to their spouse what is sexually pleasing to them. The spouse needs to be clear on his wife's likes or dislikes, and what areas in the bedroom need fixing.

In addition, I would recommend compromising in areas that you feel comfortable in compromising in. In other words, don't do anything that will cause you to lower your standards or your morals. Know what makes you comfortable and happy, and tell your spouse. Both of you have to make each other happy and find ways to please each other sexually. As equally important as sexual pleasure, is making sure your spouse knows how much you value and appreciate him. Tell him often how much you love him, as it will definitely improve the level of physical intimacy, and draw you two closer together. Speak life into each other and show your expressions of love, appreciation, commitment, dedication and loyalty to each other through inward and outward affections. Overall, married couples need to establish a strong, healthy, fulfilled, long-lasting marriage.

CASE STUDY # 3:

Teonna (sister) and Robert Mills III (brother-in-law) have been married for thirteen years, and are in their upper-thirties.

Question: We will discuss on separation. What brought you back together after a separation? Why did you separate in the first place and later decide to remain together?

Robert's Response: My wife asked me to leave, believing that the time apart would be good for us. She believed that we had grown apart and wanted different things in life. We openly discussed about getting a divorce and making the separation permanent. It was difficult at first, but I learned to adjust to being single and married simultaneously. However, I missed not being able to interact with my children daily. I was not sure if it would be temporary or a process we had to work through on the path to reconciliation.

Teonna's Response: I asked Robert to leave because I felt that we were on two different paths. I did not believe that we could work things out. I felt that the ideals of marriage and raising children from Robert's point of view were eccentric and just plain foolish. He didn't like being questioned and I had many questions. To me, I was allowing him to come to his senses and spend time alone with God. He could pray and truly reflect on what he really wanted in his life. I had already been praying and continued to pray in peace.

Knowing that God hates divorce and the effects it has on the family, we reconciled with a pledge to correct the things that led to the separation. Initially, we worked hard to revive the marriage and our relationship. Sometimes, we fall back into the same patterns as before. But when it's all said and done, we love God, each other, and our family. This is why we fight so hard to stay together and to remain in God's will.

Author's Perspective: I have said this so many times before and I will repeat it again. There is power in unity. Sometimes, you may have to separate from your spouse to work on getting that power back in your marriage. Oftentimes, God will separate you so that you can see yourself for who you are in order to work on your personal issues. When you are blinded by the other's faults, you are unable to see your own. At times, separation can strengthen your marriage.

Distance makes a heart grow fonder. Sometimes, distance can perform miracles in your marriage as it allows you to reflect and self-examine yourself. However, don't make it a lengthy separation. Separate for a time and season, then you must come together to work on the marriage. Only separate long enough to clearly see what the problems were, so you can work on those problems and discover solutions together.

God doesn't honor divorce, so you should do everything you can to salvage the marriage. However, it will not work if one of you gives up on making it work. Both of you have to come to an agreement that the marriage can be saved, then save it. There is power in unity because a two-strand cord cannot be easily broken and when you add God to the equation, then no man will be able to separate what God has put together. Allow God to minister to the both of you during your time of separation and continue to talk with each other to resolve your issues.

Keeping the communication alive is so important towards putting the marriage back together again. No marriage is perfect and there will be problems. Sometimes, separation is necessary, but again, do not have a lengthy time of separation so that you don't allow the enemy to bridge a wider gap than he already has. Separate for a short period of time. During this time, both of you need to talk, pray, meditate, and take an assessment in the retrospection of the past and then come back together for a resolution. God put you two together, so you should stay together if at all possible. At times, divorce is necessary. If there is power in unity, there is power in physical intimacy. God gives us both. Therefore, use them to your advantage.

CASE STUDY #4:

My parents, Annie and Vermon Sheppard have been married for fifty years, and are in their late sixties and early seventies.

Question: How did you stay married for so long and have you ever thought about leaving? What are both of your strengths and weaknesses?

Annie's Response (my Mom): Vermon and I were married on June 15, 1960, when I was eighteen years old. Your father was twenty-two. My mom died when I was twelve years old. Your daddy was the only man that my dad would allow to come and see me. Your granddaddy Ocie trusted your dad because he worked with him. I was pregnant with my first daughter, Sherry, before I married your father. Granddaddy Ocie said that I had to leave the house and get married.

I thought about leaving your daddy several times because I had a difficult time raising my thirteen children on a low income. I remember being left on the side of the road several times because your father's car had broken down. I recall struggling many times and doing without on many occasions for my children to have things for school.

I didn't leave because of my marriage vow to God that I would stay until death do us part. Your daddy is a good man, but he did not know his responsibilities as a man. He was not taught. The only thing he learned was the Bible. While the other children were in the library reading, your father was in a corner reading his Bible.

He was sort of slow in his learning abilities because he only read the Bible.

He had a good attitude, very calm person, likable personality, and all his teachers admired him. I give your father credit for your spiritual upbringing and also helping financially, but I also provided financial support and gave the emotional support. I am blessed to have all my children because I know God is with me because I had no momma to go to for help.

Author's Perspective: Yes, I can understand what my mother is talking about when it came to struggling and surviving as a family. I remember vividly working in the peach and okra fields, to help my parents out with the bills. Actually, all twelve of my siblings had to work in the fields when we were growing up. We didn't have a choice. I also remember those times when we ran out of heat several times during the coldest days of the winter. It was so cold. My mom was furious at my daddy. She fussed at him and cursed, until he had to go somewhere to get us some heat. He bought this little small, wooden gas heater that would last probably one week and he got it re-filled until he had enough money to fill up the big tank with gas.

Aside from what my mom said daddy didn't do, I remember my father waking us up every morning at 5:30 a.m. for our school days. I also remember my daddy coming into our bedrooms and turning on the heat about thirty minutes before we woke up for school, so we were warm while getting dressed for school. We got ready for school, without feeling freezing cold.

I recall my daddy making sure we all attended church every Sunday. Even when we complained about not wanting to go or not having anything to wear, we went. We went during a time when my mom was not even going to church, but daddy went and so did we. Not only did we go to church, we were all actively involved in church duties. We all sang in the choir, participated in Easter and Christmas plays, or any activities the church had, we did. My father knew the Word of God. He loves the Lord. To this day, my daddy is active in church. Even though we only live three minutes away from the church, my daddy would get to church at least thirty minutes before everyone else. He would be the first one there and the last one to leave. My momma hated it. But, that was my daddy. He was never, ever late for anything. You could always count on him.

I also remember my daddy taking me almost every day to cheerleading practice, without complaining. (I was a cheerleader my senior year of high school.) He did it. I also remember that I loved the chocolate candy bar made by Hershey's called *Whatchamacallit* and every time when my daddy went to the store, he bought me one. I still love that chocolate candy bar today. So, those types of things are what I remember about my father. Yes, we struggled as a family. I know that my mom had a hard time raising all thirteen of us because she didn't have a mom or a father for support, but daddy was there. Our paternal grandmother was available too. She was our guardian angel.

Daddy stayed through the good, bad, and rough times, and even when momma wanted to turn in the towel, daddy stayed. Even when momma fussed, yelled, and cursed at daddy, he stayed. Therefore, I am sure at times daddy wanted to leave all of us too, but he never said anything. He had a quiet, calming spirit about him. He only got upset when he was at his breaking point. He was the calmest one in the midst of our storms. Moreover, he knew Jesus Christ and made sure his children knew Him too. This is the foundation we needed to be where we are today. I tell you these things because of how valuable and important family is in your relationships. You can tell a lot about a person based on his family's background. The key to knowing him is to know his family.

CONCLUSION

We know what foreplay is truly about. It's more than rose petals and bubble baths, but it is about achieving the level of intimacy that will connect you with your future spouse on a deeper and meaningful level. It's about *making love* because any two people can have sex, but it takes establishing intimacy to make love. So, this entire book was about foreplay, which is essentially making love. Did you all get that? Hopefully by now, you clearly understand the difference between having sex and making love. Connecting on the spiritual and emotional side of a person's being through prayer, praise, participation, promise/potential, passion, etc. is all about making love. When the sex is over, then what? Can you still get along with him and have a great conversation after the sex is over? After the sex is over, do you still "like" him or are you only getting your needs met? After the sex, do you still have a lively relationship or do you dislike everything he does? Do you really have a lot in common after all? Be honest with yourself.

Please, think about these things and see what you know about the person you're sleeping with. If you are a person who believes in your value, then allow God to provide the best man who will treat you with dignity, respect, love, care, and consideration. He will know the difference between **making love** to you versus **having sex** with you.

Let's not worry about how much money he has because a godly man will do what he has to do to take care of you and his family, even if he has to work two jobs. He knows a queen needs to be treated like one. The key is that you have to first treat yourself like a queen to show him how you desire to be treated. If you don't live like one, he won't treat you like one. Now, I am not talking about materialistic or worldly possessions at all in reference to "he needs to treat you like a queen," but what I am speaking on is your presentation. Know your value and self-worth and don't settle for anything less than God's best. Remember ladies, you are the chase.

We're too caught up in things of the world. *Romans 12:2 reads, "And do not be conformed to this world, but be transformed by the renewing of your mind, that you may prove what is that good and acceptable and perfect will of God."* We have allowed the worldly ways to be in us, not allowing God to work in us. When we shift our focus more on God and less on ourselves, then God will give us the desires of our heart.

I hope these eleven principles and practical applications with dissecting the life of Job helped you evaluate your relationships. I hope the thought-provoking questions challenged you in your thinking and how you approach your relationships and I hope that my family's testimonies helped you in some way or another. Also, the six ideas for married couples to achieve greater intimacy will hopefully begin to come alive in their marriage. Hopefully, you will approach things differently now since you have gained wisdom and insight on what it is God is telling you to focus your attention on. It's not about the quantity, but about quality. No matter how many people you sleep with, you will still not achieve real intimacy until you grasp these eleven keys outlined in this book and apply them. Think about the way you viewed sex and how you handled yourself. Sex is a wonderful experience that is meant to be shared between a husband and a wife. If you care about the quality of your relationship, then hopefully this book has guided you in that direction.

Now that you have been equipped with the tools needed to have a healthy, quality, and fulfilled relationship, I believe you are ready to turn off the lights. All throughout this book, I gave you keys that you needed to put in place before you turned off the lights. Now that you know what to do before those lights go off, you will have a great long-lasting marriage.

This last bit of advice is for **married couples ONLY**. Singles, I have something special for you at the end of the book, so stay with me.

Married couples, you have the green light to do what God made to be special, beautiful, wonderful, and a thrilling experience—to enjoy making love to your spouse. I thought of this particular song because it fits with my title. Teddy Pendergrass' song, *Turn off the Lights* tells you exactly what to do. Here are some of the lyrics:

> Turn off the lights and light a candle
> Tonight, I'm in a romantic mood, yeah
> Let's take a shower, shower together, yeah
> I'll wash your body and you'll wash mine, yeah
> Rub me down in some hot oils baby, yeah
> And I'll do the same thing to you

I'm going to stop right here as there is no need to go any further. You got it. **Make sure you have all these keys in place before those lights go out and remember the lights only go out if you are married.**

The things which you learned and received and heard and saw in me, these do, and the God of peace will be with you. Philippians 4:7. Be blessed. I love you and God loves you even more.

P.S. Remember when I started this book, I told you this book was NOT about sex. Well, it wasn't, was it?

AFTERWORD

For the single men and women: I believe now is the perfect time to put all the things that we have learned from this book into action. Faith without works is dead so I would like you to put your faith to the test and pose to you a covenant challenge.

Throughout this book, we talked about how to achieve real physical intimacy in your relationships. We have also learned that it is not only about sex, but also connecting to the emotional and spiritual side of your being. The eleven principles outlined in this book will help you achieve the level of intimacy that has been missing in your relationships, whether you are single, dating, or married. These principles are for everyone. I also posed challenging questions to help you ponder on what areas in your relationship that may need more attention and some pointers to the married couples on those things they can implement right now to increase the intimacy in their marriage.

Now, I would like to shift gears a bit and pose a challenge to the single men and women, whether you are dating or not, to accept this pre-marital covenant challenge. For the next six months, I am asking 1000 men and women to volunteer sacrificially to practice abstinence and celibacy as a promise-covenant to God. My primary target is for unmarried couples that are in recent and committed relationships who want to experience a life-changing transformation with God.

I chose six months since during this time span of dating, this is the period where a serious commitment evolves such as an engagement. In six months, you should definitely have a firm grasp on where the relationship is headed or should be headed. Additionally, you should know whether or not this is the right type of person for you. I know some of you move faster in your relationships than others, but I believe that six months is a sufficient timeframe to make a lifetime commitment with someone. Therefore, once your relationship makes the six month mark, then the both of you should be discussing a long-term commitment— marriage.

Now, we are ready to step into the "pre-marital stages" over a six month period. I will give you twelve steps to keep your covenant commitment with the 12 step abstinence program and Scripture readings to stay on task, and finally offer you the covenant challenge that will change your life as well as enhance your relationships forever.

PRE-MARITAL RELATIONSHIP STAGES:

Before we get into the six month covenant challenge that we are doing collectively, I have put together a brief timeline of what I believe will take place in the six months duration of your initial meeting with the covenant-promise. This may vary by individual, but overall, this is where you need to be or should be in the course of your relationship. Take the self-examination to see why, if you are not, and discover where you should be. Feel free to keep a journal of your feelings, emotions, triumph, downfalls, and so forth to keep track of your daily progress, which has been provided for you as an addition to this book. Writing is therapeutic and is also a learning tool.

1ˢᵗ month: This is the stage where you are strictly getting to know the other person. Talking on the phone, texting, and emailing are some things you do in this stage as a way of becoming acquainted with one another. You also acquire communication techniques favorable with each other, and how the other person thinks. If most of your conversations are geared towards sex, then he/she is not talking in the manner that meets your standards, so there is no need to go any further. He/she does not value your worth. You can stress to your significant other where you stand in this relationship, if he does not abide to your standards and refuse to follow through; it is time to end this short-term acquaintance. Moreover, the relationship will not work so don't waste any more time than you already have.

2ⁿᵈ month: This is stage where you have face-to-face interactions. You accept his invitation to go out on a date. You have a better understanding about each other and discover any physical attractions for the other person. This physical attraction or chemistry will help to determine whether or not the relationship will work. Don't focus only on the physical aspects, but also on personality and character. Finding out more about each other's likes and dislikes happens in this stage. This is the getting to "know me" stage.

3ʳᵈ month: This is the stage where you are still dating and getting to know each other better. At this stage, you are learning about each other's family background and upbringing. Personal communication is involved and much deeper and intimate. You are asking the tough questions such as finding out medical history, spiritual life, educational status, child-bearing and parental skills, and family values and beliefs.

4ᵗʰ month: This is the stage where you meet each other's families, children, and close relatives and friends. You are confident in your relationship and have a strong sense that it is solid. You can see this as a long lasting relationship. In other words, you are serious about making a commitment to him because you will not meet the family until you firmly believe that he/she is the right one. Try to avoid going into this act prematurely. You do not want to expose your family and children to any man or woman whom you are "dating at the moment". Do not seek a rebound-relationship if this one does not work after three or four months of the courtship stage. In other words, do not bring anyone else into your personal space until you are ready for a serious commitment. The desire to have sex happens in this stage as well as talking a lot about sex. Remember to set guidelines or boundaries to reiterate where you stand as you had indicated in the beginning of your "getting to know me" phrase, which was mentioned in stage one and two.

5th month: This is the stage where you are definitely in a serious, committed relationship. In other words, you don't want or desire anyone else. You have found the right person. At this stage, you are clearly in love and thinking about each other all the time. You hate being apart or away from him/her over a short period of time. You are in love with each other in the fourth month (stage) after meeting the families. From this day forth, you know your divine connection and feelings for one another. You are constantly thinking about one another, missing each other when apart, and enjoying each other's company in this stage.

6th month: This is the stage where engagement should take place. Even if you are not engaged to be married in this stage, you are headed in this direction. The promise to get married should take place in this stage. Otherwise, you would have wasted your time and energy on a relationship where he/she wants to be with you, but not ready to marry you. This is also the stage where the pressure to have sex is evident. Now that he has held out for six months, he might want you to have sex to seal the relationship or reward him for waiting. Don't give in. You have sacrificed six months to demonstrate your covenant-promise to God and prayed to wait until your wedding night. If he is not ready to marry you and unwilling to wait to have sex, then he may not be the one for you.

This stage will also clearly define any doubts you may have had about his commitment to you and see if he will constantly pressure you for sex. It is possible that the relationship could end in this stage because the two of you are not on the same page. You want someone who is committed to marriage. He says that he will marry you in the future, so we can have sex now since you will be his wife. Stand firm and confident in your belief, and know your value and know you are worth the wait. If he cannot wait for you, then he is not worthy to be with you. God blesses those who wait and endure to the end. He saves the best for last. He also says in His Word that being last is first in God's eyes. As long as you finish the race, it doesn't matter what place you come in. The key to the race is finishing it—believe you can finish.

TWELVE STEPS TO PRACTICING ABSTINENCE/CELIBACY FOR YOUR COVENANT CHALLENGE:

Step 1: Minimal Physical Contact

Keep any physical contact to a minimum and limited only to hugging, holding hands, a peck on the lips, and no massages. Avoiding physical contact will help you in the long run. The more physical contacts we allow to transpire, the harder it will be to practice abstinence or celibacy. Don't set ourselves up for failure. Respect our bodies and establish guidelines by telling the person upfront. Once we acknowledge in the beginning of establishing a friendship that we're practicing abstinence or celibacy, then they can make the decision to abide to our standards or leave. We are devoted and committed to follow-through the guidelines that God has set forth for us when it comes to keeping our bodies pure. Therefore, we let our significant others know from the very beginning where we stand.

Step 2: Avoid Temptation Advances

Resist sexual temptation by saying "no" and run when confronted with it. Let our actions speak louder than our words. We have to resist the devil and he will flee. Sometimes we have to do as Joseph did when he was confronted with temptation from Potiphar's wife—he ran. With destiny and purpose, we are willing to do whatever it takes to fulfill the promise of God set for our lives. One bad decision can change the course of our life. Make the decision when faced with the sexual temptation to flee from it or avoid it. Desperate people, like Joseph, do desperate things to protect their purpose and destiny. See Genesis 39:7.

Step 3: Encourage Yourself
We have to encourage *ourselves* while undergoing sexual purity. We have to speak positive things into our spirit. Once we speak these things aloud, we are able to do it and the Word of God tells us that we are more than conquerors. We have the power of life and death in our tongue; so speak life and not a word of defeat into our atmosphere. We also have to motivate ourselves and speak those things that are not as if they already are.

Step 4: Bring Others on the Date
Go out on double dates. It is best to be surrounded with friends and family members to avoid being pressured when alone. If we are alone together, make it an early dinner and watch a movie, and ask him/her to leave. Also, set a curfew of the exact time he/she needs to leave your home and strictly stick with what you have set and established. We have to follow the rules we set for ourselves if we want others to follow them. Our primary goal is to avoid any sexual contact. In a serious commitment, we cannot allow anything to deter us from our focus. Don't let anything stand in our way. Flee from sexual temptation at all costs. Date in public and not in private to help us deter from being caught up in the "heat of the moment."

Step 5: Be Honest About Your Feelings and Thoughts
Remain honest and upfront with each other about our feelings and emotions. Honesty tells our partner where we stand in the relationship. Too many relationships go

sour because of dishonesty, or not sharing our true intentions. We shouldn't hide or avoid our feelings. We can make things worse by concealing our true intentions because sexual temptation becomes stronger to bear as Satan will use our silence and subconscious feelings to add suggestions to our thought-process. Avoid clichés, false expressions and sayings, and wearing a mask with our significant others because they deserve to see the *real you*. This person can be our future husband. Keep it real. *Hint:* Couples need to be on the same page for this to work by being open and upfront in order to discuss ways that help each other from sexual temptation. This method will allow us to speak openly, honestly, and overcome sexual temptations. Share with each other our boundaries, weaknesses, and turn-on's so we know which buttons not to push.

Step 6: Know You

We have to know who we are sexually, meaning what turns us on. We have to know our weaknesses, failures, past mistakes, and what tempts us. For instance, if soft music puts us in the mood for sexual contact, then we shouldn't play any romantic music in our significant others' presence. Kissing may turn us on too, so we have to know our limitations and know how far we should go before anything happens that we don't want to happen. We know what our fleshly desires are, so at all costs, don't let the flesh win. We have submitted to our fleshly desires in the past. We have pleaded and asked God to help us defeat this giant in our life and he will help us, but we also have to make wise, sound decisions in our dating. We can not put ourselves in uncompromising positions where we are vulnerable and allow our weaknesses to overtake us. For example, being alone in their apartment watching a romantic comedy and going past the curfew time we have set for them will put us in a situation where we may not be able to control our sexual urges. We know that there's something sensual and sexual about nighttime that puts us in a mood to engage in sex because nighttime means it's time for bed. Combine that with watching sexual images on television and our mind will automatically think about sex and our body will react. Again, it is so important that we recognize our sexual peaks and avoid them at all costs.

Step 7: Seek God through Prayer
Prayer is the key to practicing abstinence or celibacy. Without prayer, we won't make it. Prayer strengthens us, sustains us, comforts us, and helps us see our fleshly desires and wants so we can turn away from them. We allow the Holy Spirit to correct us and refine us. God will help us, but we first have to ask Him. Therefore, pray to God for the discipline, faith, and strength to sustain.

Prayer helps me to safeguard my purity because God imparts His Holy Spirit inside of me to mend those areas where I am weak. The Bible tells us that God's strength is made perfect in our weakness. Therefore, I turn over my weaknesses to Him in exchange for His strengths. We will not survive this covenant journey without God in our corner, so pray without ceasing. Not only pray, we are also to fast and read God's Word.

Step 8: Refocus on Your Purpose
Refocus means to shift our focus towards positive things, not negative. Think about our goals, dreams, and ideas and begin implementing them. We need to begin praying about our purpose and destiny because this will

take our mind off of our flesh. We also need to work diligently on our dreams and goals because working on them requires time and effort and the more we exert towards those things, the less time we have to spend thinking about our sexual desires. When we begin to work on God's plan and desires He has already set for us, our sexual desires will be less of a struggle for us because our attention will shift from our flesh to our purpose. Our sexual desires will not fade away completely and we don't want them to because we will need them for marriage, but what we desire is to control those urges. Once we do that, it will not be as difficult as it was before to refrain from sex because our desires have shifted towards our purpose.

Step 9: Be mindful of what we *see*, *hear* and *read*.
What we feed into our spirit will have a direct impact on the way we view sex. These images in our mind cause us to start lusting for someone after what we've seen. This happened to David. He lusted after Bathsheba by watching her too long with his eyes while she was bathing. He slept with a married woman in which lead to the murder of her husband in order to be with her (See *2 Samuel 11*). All of this happened because David saw her naked and stared too long, and allowed his sexual arousals to take a hold of him. Get rid of any sexual objects or sexually explicit materials such as magazines, books, tapes, DVDs, and CDs. We can't just put them away in a closet because later we will be tempted to play them or look at them. So, we should discard them completely. We are to put action behind our words and not just talk about it, but actually do things to show we are committed to Christ.

Step 10: Remain Active and Proactive

Stay busy and active in any extracurricular activities or ministry functions. Once we are actively involved in these activities, there will be less time to meditate on sex. As a couple, it is best to plan things together and help each other in the covenant challenge. We can also volunteer our time and service. Voluntary activities are for a good cause and will also keep our minds off sex. Additionally, many people find their purpose and passion through volunteer services. Volunteering allows us to discover what we enjoy doing in our community and helping others. Don't fill our calendar days with frivolous things, but do things that pleases God and as a couple. An idle mind is the devil's workshop so refuse to be idle and stagnant. Stay focused and moving forward.

Step 11: Place Restrictions on Seeing Each Other

This may come off a little harsh and probably the most difficult suggestion; however, our quality time spent together needs to be safeguarded. *Safeguards* are also putting restrictions on how close we become and engaged while in each other's company. I can not stress this enough, but we also have to limit our physical contact. I know this step is hard because when we get in a committed relationship, we will want to see our significant other on a regular basis. We are inclined to temptation when we spend a lot of time together alone. Distance helps us refrain from sexual temptation and also makes our relationship stronger and fonder. This will test the strength of the relationship and our commitment. There are two options: either this will drive them away or draw them closer. Our partners will respect and value our commitment to God. Only do this act when it's confirmed that this is a solid and steady relationship because trust has been established.

When God says he/she is the one, this person will remain for the long haul, for better and worse. If not, he/she will surely leave to find the mate God has ordained for him. It is best to know where a person's heart is at this very moment than finding out later when feelings have flourished. Some relationships will not endure because of the time apart, but it's worth the try. Besides seeing him three times a week, it may be best to reduce it to twice a week. Send texts, or pictures via phone, talking hours at a time on the phone or via Skype, and social communication on Facebook, Myspace, Twitter, or whatever social networks because of the distance and unable to see face-to-face. There are so many things to tell or show the person in a committed relationship how much you care for them; yet, our main focus is to please God.

Step 12: Associate with Positive, Like-Minded People
Lastly, one of the most important steps is to connect with positive, uplifting people. One of my favorite scriptures in the Bible is *Proverbs 27:17, "as iron sharpens iron, so a man sharpens the countenance of his friend."* It is critical to our well-being and growth to surround ourselves with people who are grounded and mature. They don't necessarily have to be Christians, but people who can encourage and uplift us and who believe in what we're trying to accomplish. Even if they aren't where we are, maybe they can help us get there and see our determination and strength to help transform and change our lives. Positive people who want to change will also influence others to do the same.

It is great to be associated with like-minded people, so we should definitely have some Christian people in our corner who are dedicated to living, holy righteous lives because they will encourage us to do the same. They will offer godly advice and encouragement to help us stay on course to practicing abstinence or celibacy. Prayer partners hold us accountable and share encouraging words to keep us focused on abstaining from sex until marriage. When we become weak or discouraged, we can call our prayer partner for prayer and encouragement on how to face temptation on those difficult days ahead. We need all the support available to us to stay dedicated to practicing abstinence or celibacy.

We once lived a life of pleasing the flesh—now it is time to be committed to God and our courtship. We once had failed relationships—now we are seeking a committed one. Why not do something differently? I promise that we will not get the same results. If we stay committed to it, then God will surely reward us. Furthermore, we have plans to make it to the wedding day. Let's imagine how great it will be? It will not be sex as usual—it will be where three unite: ourselves, him, and God.

As a disclaimer, I would like to explicitly state that this twelve step program is NOT designed to take away our desire for sex, but to control those desires so we do not succumb to them by engaging in pre-marital sex or fornication, which is a sin according to the Bible. We still want to desire sex so we can desire our future spouses. When we take control over our flesh, it doesn't mean that we won't think about sex or don't want to have sex. It only means that we are no longer controlled or hindered by our sexual desires. When we let go of our desires, God will put His desire for us inside us so that we will be on one accord with Him. When we do God's will, He will give us the desires of our heart. God made every human being with sexual desires, but His will is for us to use those desires when we get married.

Many of us have always been in relationships and currently have an active sex life, so to change it now will be difficult, but not impossible. I'm suggesting that we stop doing what we are currently doing and try something new. We first must change our thinking and then our actions will change. This program is for those who want to start their lives fresh and who want to change their behavior.

I hope these twelve steps will help us remain committed to our goal. I want to help us in any way to get to the finish line. The choice is really up to us. If we are ready and willing to change, then God is ready and willing to help us along the way. He only needs a willing vessel. We can do it. I believe we can. I know we will. I will be praying and cheering that we will finish this journey successfully together. We have to start first by putting sex on the backburner, and placing more emphasis on establishing an emotional and spiritual connection, which is what this book is all about. I hope you are ready to take this challenge as I am. I have been successfully practicing abstinence for years and it has been hard, but everyday I do it and so can you. At the end of thirty-one years old, I am still a virgin. I couldn't have done it alone. God helped me every step of the way and He will help you too. God bless you.

P.S. There is also a free resource guide in addition to this book that will help you with your covenant challenge. Please go to my website at: www.iamthechase.com to download the free guide. The guide is called "Walking the Path to Real Love: 12 Steps to Practice Abstinence or Celibacy."

Key Scriptures to Ponder Along
Your Covenant Journey:

Read *Psalm 23.*

"I can do all things through Christ who strengthens me" (Philippians 4:13).

"One thing have I desired of the Lord, that will I seek [after]; that I may dwell in the house of the Lord all the days of my life, to behold the beauty of the Lord, and to inquire in His temple" (Psalm 27:4, author's translation).

"The righteous cry, and the Lord hears, and delivers them out of all their troubles" (Psalm 34:17).

"As the deer pants after the water brooks, so pants my soul for You, O God" (Psalm 42:1).

"There is therefore now no condemnation to them who are in Christ Jesus, who walk not after the flesh, but according to the Spirit" (Romans 8:1).

"I beseech you therefore, brethren, by the mercies of God, that you present your bodies a living sacrifice, holy, acceptable to God, which is your reasonable service" (Romans 12:1).

"My grace is sufficient for you, for My strength is made perfect in weakness" (2 Corinthians 12:9, author's translation).

"Now to Him who is able to do exceedingly abundantly above all that we ask or think, according to the power that works in us" (Ephesians 3:20).

"And let us not grow weary while doing good, for in due season we shall reap if we do not lose heart [faint not]" (Galatians 6:9, author's translation).

THE PRE-MARITAL COVENANT CHALLENGE BETWEEN YOU AND GOD:

This is a six month covenant challenge. I would like to offer this challenge to those who are willing, accountable, and accepting to abide to God's pre-marital covenant. I am asking 1000 single men and women to step into a spiritual realm, a covenant with God, for six months of practicing abstinence or celibacy. *Abstinence* (www.dictionary.com) is any self-restraint, self-denial, or forbearance. We are restraining from any sexual contact, activities, and any types of sexual objects such as pornography, masturbation, oral sex, etc. *Celibacy* (www.dictionary.com) is abstention from sexual relations; abstention by vow from marriage; and the stage of being unmarried. We are not succumbing to our lustful, sexual desires with our committed partner. We will flee from any fornication just as Joseph did when Potiphar's wife had a sexual attraction for Joseph. Even if we are physically attracted to someone else, we will still flee from the temptation. I believe that Joseph had an attraction with Potiphar's wife, which is another reason why he ran. He knew his covenant with God and the purpose God placed inside him, so he ran from the temptation. (See *Genesis 39:7*).

If you have any questions or comments concerning this faith challenge to live a life of abstinence or celibacy for these next six months, please email me directly to inform me so I can be praying with you and for you. We are all in this Christian walk together. I am determined to finish my race and develop a closer relationship with God, and also have a sincere intimate relationship with my future spouse. If you are committed to do the pre-marital covenant challenge, email me at: covenantchallenge@gmail.com, and write in the subject line: Pre-marital Covenant Challenge. I want to count you in! Review my site at www.iamthechase.com to register for the challenge. You can also contact me throughout your progress via Twitter at Dladyque or Facebook page (Quiniece Sheppard). I need a minimum of 1000 single men and women to make this commitment today. Whether we are in a current relationship or single, I am challenging us to be in a pre-marital covenant for six months starting today. Who's in?

During the six month timeframe, I will be praying for you and sending daily inspirational emails to encourage our faith walk. This is a walk of faith to deny our flesh, to commit to holy and righteous living for six full months. Don't do it for me, but do it for yourself and for your relationship with God. I am hopeful that when we agree to this covenant challenge, not only will we have completed the task and kept our covenant-promise to God and to ourselves, but we would have also succeeded in the area of our flesh and gained the supernatural ability to defeat temptation.

In Steve Harvey's book, *Act like a Lady and Think like a Man*, he suggested to give your man a 90-day trial period before engaging in sex. I disagree with this statement because it is not biblical. The Bible states that we are not to take part in fornication and forbids pre-marital sex.

1 Corinthians 6:13 reads, *"Now the body is not for fornication, but for the Lord and the Lord for the body."*

The purpose of this challenge is to deny our flesh from all sexual activities for six months, or until marriage. Again, all sexual activities include oral sex, masturbation, pornography, or any other sexual act that involves sex.

Philippians 4:13* reads, *"I can do all things through Christ who strengthens me."

We can do it! It will take prayer, meditation, fasting, and wholehearted commitment on our part. I will be there with you every step of the way to help us keep our covenant. If you are serious, then so is God. He is ready to help us do this. All God needs is an invitation.

Please sign and date and tear off this page and paste it somewhere you can see it daily as a reminder of your commitment to God and yourself.
****

I accept this six month covenant challenge and will value my body as a living temple for the Lord. I will commit to not indulging in sexual activities and lustful desires—surrender it over to God. After the six month covenant challenge, I will continue to do my best to live a life that is pleasing to God and will abstain from sex until marriage.

Signed: _____

Dated: _____

Now, we have declared with our signature that we will start with our promise-covenant with God. Our *day one* is the first day we start, whether it is the next day after we read this book or two weeks later or even six months from now. Whenever we decide to take on the challenge, then this is our day one. A journal is included in addition to this book to help us keep track of our progress.

This is such a difficult task for many, since some of us have higher sex drives than others. Therefore, we may relapse after one full week. Some may be able to survive a month without any sexual contact. I encourage you to start over again. Don't give in. Donnie McClurkin tells us in his song, "We fall down, but we get back up again." Don't look at falling down as defeat, but look at it as a way of making us stronger.

God's strength is made perfect in our weakness. When we are at our weakest point is when God is at His strongest. We need to rely on His strength to see us through this challenge. Whether we start over five times or twenty times, it doesn't matter to God. What's important to God is that we finish the race, not where we start. Remember this: *"...Let us run with endurance [patience] the race that is set before us, looking unto Jesus, the author and finisher of our faith" (Hebrews 12:1-2). Ecclesiastes 9:11 reads, "I returned and saw under the sun that—the race is not to the swift, nor the battle to the strong...but time and chance happens to them all."*

Please fill out the information at the bottom of this book and mail it back to me. You can also fill out the form at my website at www.iamthechase.com and click on: **Covenant Challenge Registration**. Or email the form to: covenant challenge@gmail.com.

You will receive a certificate of achievement and accomplishment for completing this challenge. Thank you and God bless you.

Name:

Age:

Sex:

Address:

Email:

Date of Completion:

ABOUT THE AUTHOR

Quiniece Sheppard is a southern girl, who grew up with twelve siblings in a rural part of Alabama. In school, Sheppard's favorite subject was English. She had a love for writing, but never dreamt of writing a book. There are two books in print now and a third book to be published in 2013. Moreover, she is excited about the books being birthed, motivational speaking opportunities, and the ministry God has assigned to her.

When God called Quiniece Sheppard into single women's ministry in 2006, she was hesitant and fearful. After the release of her first book in 2009, titled *The Seven Deadly Sexual Sins*, she trusted and obeyed God. Her desire is to encourage single young women to practice abstinence and celibacy and continue to believe in their faith. She also wants to encourage their self-esteem, confidence level, and to have a clearer understanding of their value and self-worth.

Many people believe that affirmation is not necessary since they know who they are already. Sheppard strongly disagrees with this statement because if you never hear about how great you are, how will you ever come to believe it? You need to hear it, so you can believe it! This is her main focus with the single women's ministry—to affirm who you are, believe in your value, and start living like a woman of destiny and purpose.

Visit www.iamthechase.com, Quiniece Sheppard's website to live out the purpose and destiny that God has placed inside of you.